NO TIME FOR LUNCH

Memoirs of an Inner City Psychologist

BY Thelma Alpert Blumberg

DEVORA PUBLISHING
JERUSALEM ◆ NEW YORK

NO TIME FOR LUNCH

Published by DEVORA PUBLISHING COMPANY

Text Copyright © 2004 by Thelma Alpert Blumberg
Cover and Book Design : Yael Kanner

Library of Congress Cataloging-in-Publication Data
Blumberg, Thelma.
No time for lunch : memoirs of a inner city psychologist / by Thelma Alpert Blumberg.
p. cm.
ISBN 1-930143-93-1 (hardcover : alk. paper) ISBN 1-932687-09-2 (paperback : alk. paper)
1. Blumberg, Thelma. 2. School psychologists – United States – Biography.
3. School psychology – United States. 4. Education, Urban – United States. I. Title.

LB3013.6.B58 2004
371.4'092--dc22
2004004613
Hard Cover   ISBN: 1-930143-93-1
Soft Cover   ISBN 1-932687-09-2

Email: publisher@devorapublishing.com
Web Site: www.devorapublishing.com

Printed in Israel

Table of Contents

To all of my loving grandchildren,
who are the frosting on the cake of life

Acknowledgments

I am most indebted to my husband, Arnold Blumberg, who not only persuaded me to write this book, but who was always there, devotedly, to consult, advise, and simplify any problems. My daughter, Rivka Livnat, and son, Raphael, were invaluable in their praise, suggestions, and encouragement upon reading the raw manuscript.

From my days of graduate school, memories of Professors Stanley Zweback and Barbara Slater are unforgettable. Their brilliant lectures on the psychology, evaluation, and counseling of children not only enhanced my work with children, but fulfilled a longing which remains useful for me until today.

I am grateful for the support of Louise Fink, whose outstanding skills were identified early in her career with the Baltimore City Schools, and who served as a supervisor of psychologists and an administrator. I view her as my mentor, as her knowledge, wisdom, and ability to simplify any confounding crisis were so helpful. I am indebted, too, to Dr. Michael Oidick, also a supervisor of psychologists, whose diagnostic skills were such that each case consultation with him proved to be a superb learning experience. In addition, over the years he was there to console me whenever I was the victim of insensitivity.

During my years of writing for *Communique'*, the monthly publication of the National Association of School Psychologists, I am appreciative for the help of the four excellent editors whom I knew. My deep thanks go to Tom Fagan, who accepted my first submission, and to Alex Thomas, who followed, and who welcomed many of my articles. To Peg Dawson, who invited me to serve as a contributing editor, an opportunity which I savored, I owe my deepest appreciation. She was followed by Andrea Canter, with whom I have had the longest and most gratifying of relationships.

Finally, I am in awe of the creative skills of my editor, Shalom Kaplan, whose editing was both instructive and motivating. His knowledge of the nuances of grammar, his patient and untiring attention to detail, and his ability to inspire, are all extraordinary. I shall forever be indebted to him for his polishing, revision, and sincere interest in my book.

Introduction

Each day for twenty-five years, my husband, a history professor, listened intently as I told him stories of events at my schools. While most of my tales were pleasant, others were stressful. But, finding all of my narratives engaging, he kept urging me, "You must write a book!"

Among my pleasing tales, one day I told him of a new teacher who came to chat with me at my office. The teacher opened her conversation by saying, "You don't remember me, do you?" Wondering who she was, I replied, " W-e-l-l, no!" She then went on to say that she had worked at the school a few years before as a teachers' aide. Relating that she used to see me bustling around the school office and corridors, her words were, "You always looked so happy!" Continuing, she told me that while she was an aide, she learned from our brief personal conversations that I had earned my college degrees after age forty. Her next words, boasting proudly, were music to my ears. She said, "You were my inspiration to return to college to earn my teaching degree."

What this teacher did not know was how improbable it actually was that she had ever come to meet me as a school psychologist. In the beginning chapters of my book, I have described my struggles to bring this about, and that it was an unlikely triumph when it did finally happen. I have titled this section, "Phase One: The Making of a School Psychologist."

While every circumstance described in these chapters played some role in shaping my calling, most significant were the problems of our profoundly handicapped son, Michael. Although it was a fact that he in no way influenced my career choice, learning to face his problems enriched me in another way. I gained wisdom, perspective, and strength to tread where others feared to go.

Phase Two embraces the bulk of the book, and is titled, "Agonies and Ecstasies." Using behavior management, a variety of eclectic theories, and just plain common sense, led me to the joy I experienced each time I helped a child, a teacher, or a parent. Prevalent here are the success stories of children whose lives I helped transform, and included too are tales of the naysayers who were always there to say "It can't be done!"

In Phase Two there are also accounts of those who were there to bully, offend, and trample on me. I have carefully disguised in every way the identities of these stressful players, usually using no names at all. I fault my own vulnerability to upstaging here, and I use these less pleasant stories to demonstrate how I matured and learned new tricks to overcome my own weakness.

I hope you will find that my tales of the magnificent children and their courageous parents are heartwarming and often amusing. There are moving tales too, of the remarkable colleagues who helped me along the way.

I felt then, and still feel, that every human contact I made in the schools opened a door to bettering the life of a child. As a corollary, it was my ardent conviction that any time wasted might sabotage the rescue of a student screaming for help. Thus the title of my book became, "No Time for Lunch."

Upon viewing my devotion to the students with whom I worked, and the fun I had while with them, my husband once clarified all of this to me in another way: "You know, the City of Baltimore pays you just to be nice!" All of us are only as successful as the happiness we make possible for others.

Thelma Alpert Blumberg

Kiryat Arba
February, 2004

PHASE ONE
Life Prepares Me

CHAPTER ONE

Kiryat Arba

"And they dwelt in the cities of Hebron, and the men of Judah came, and there they anointed David king."

II Samuel 2:12

Here we are enjoying retirement in Kiryat Arba, Israel! Only a short distance away is Hebron, known as the "cradle of Jewish History." Our biblical ancestors Abraham, Sarah, Isaac, Rebecca, Jacob and Leah – all rest there in the burial caves known as the Machpelah.

It may seem strange that I begin the story of my adventure as a psychologist at its last chapter, instead of at its beginning. Nevertheless, there is no way to explore what I have done with my years as a psychologist without peeking at the end. We can go back to the beginning after we have seen the ending.

Kiryat Arba itself is an enchanting town with colorful, vibrant gardens and immaculately clean streets, all designed and cared for by its devoted citizens. The six thousand people living here, from diverse parts of the world, depict an ingathering of a most extraordinary group of Jews.

Even before retirement as a school psychologist at the Baltimore City schools, we spent our summers in Kiryat Arba, visiting our son and his family. I became captivated then by the unique and dedicated people who chose to live here. My fascination with the people was only natural, as the study of all human behavior is the essence of my very being.

"Uri the Felafel Man" was one who caught my attention quickly. Whenever visiting Kiryat Arba, we paid regular visits to Uri Dror's felafel stand, and I noted that although other felafel vendors had come and gone, yet Uri's was always there. It was a known fact his felafel was reliably delicious, a just cause for survival.

Looking at Uri's primitive shack, however, made one wonder. After business hours, when his six-by-eight stand was closed, it looked like a homemade, scrap metal shelter, surrounded by huge rocks and boulders. I was amazed to learn that Uri had no running water and that he managed by carrying tubs from across the street. I always felt reassured, though, when I saw him out front each evening, spending what seemed like hours scrubbing his large pots. When the stand was open, a telephone was visible, an incongruous sight amid the unsophisticated and crude surroundings.

The entire establishment was really an eyesore, and it was rumored that the town fathers of picturesque Kiryat Arba debated whether to take measures to close it. After all, they took much pride in their charming town, with its neatly landscaped subtropical plants and its multicolored flower beds.

One summer, however, I saw an unbelievable sight! On the land behind Uri's falafel stand, a beautiful one-story building, resplendent with numerous arches and a large open veranda, was being built. I learned that this was Uri's project, the future location for his felafel business. Becoming very interested in this paradoxical sight, I quickly photographed the old shanty and the blossoming new building, side by side.

On another visit, I was thrilled to see the old shack gone, and standing there was the newly built, radiant white building! Inside was every modern convenience, along with its triumphantly announced menu. Both inside and out on the covered terrace were a number of white tables. When bus drivers passed by it was not unusual to hear them honk their horns, and then to see Uri come running out with one of his "special" sandwiches.

Beside myself with joy and wonderment at this miraculous transformation, I thought I must explore further how it all came about. That it took place at a time of political unrest intrigued me most. Uri was flattered by the interest shown by this strange American woman, and his amazing story emerged.

Uri, then sixty years old, was the son of Iraqi parents who migrated to Palestine in the nineteen-twenties. For twenty-five years he and his wife had been living in Kiryat Arba, where they raised their son and daughter, and engaged in the felafel business. At the same time he served bravely as a reservist in the Israeli army, defending his country during the '56 Sinai campaign, and the Six Day and Yom Kippur wars.

"This new building has been my long standing, dormant dream" he revealed. "I knew it was now or never, and that pushed me even harder. Yes, there were political hassles and anxious days while the mortgage cleared and the building permits were granted."

14

Kiryat Arba

Remarkably, Uri's persistence triumphed! Today, just a twenty-five minute walk from the burial place of the Biblical Patriarchs and Matriarchs, stands the splendid symbol of his courage.

On another summer visit, in those years before retirement, my ears pricked up when I was introduced to school psychologist Levy Van Leeuwen. As he was a resident of Kiryat Arba and serviced the schools there, I was delighted when he agreed to an interview. Meeting him was a rare find, as his training and position mirrored my own in the Baltimore community. Yet, what I learned from his experiences far surpassed any expectations I may have had.

It was of special interest to hear of Van Leeuwen's work with the Ethiopian Jewish students and their families, a minority within the Kiryat Arba community. He discussed the Ethiopians with obvious fascination and deep affection. His comments about the students were inspiring.

It would be expected that the problems of any population rescued from the perils of war, after long years of starvation, such as the Ethiopians were, would create an undeniable challenge. Yet these students are highly intelligent, diligent, and avid for education. They strive to enter the universities and to do well in the army. They excel in math skills, and even those who had no prior schooling, quickly learn complex math concepts, and how to use computers.

Van Leeuwen described a visit, on a windy, rainy winter day, to an Ethiopian Jewish home in Kiryat Arba, where the heat was not working. While all the family lay huddled under blankets, a nine-year-old girl sat on the icy stone floor. She was doing her homework so intently that she appeared oblivious to the cold.

It would be dishonest to pretend that the racial and cultural differences of these children do not affect them. Van Leeuwen related that on one occasion, a fifth-grade girl flatly refused to go on a class trip to the seashore. When questioned about it, she responded, "I don't need to go to the beach, I am already dark enough!"

Van Leeuwen described the Ethiopian Jews as gentle, pleasant, and passive. In their desire to integrate they are sometimes eager to shake off some of their customs, as the challenges to adjustment – social, cultural, and economic – can be overwhelming. Yet it is rare for these gentle people to turn to crime or drugs in their frustration. All in all, the Ethiopian Jews of Kiryat Arba appear to be making a good adjustment, and to be on the path to becoming a distinct asset to the patch-quilt population of the nation of Israel.

As retirees now living in Kiryat Arba we enjoy being among the fresh, newest symbols of courage, the Jewish emigres from the late Soviet Union. Among them are the highly educated, who already hold advanced university degrees. They struggle and succeed with learning Hebrew quickly, and undergo retraining in their professions. My own physician, Dr. Slobodnik, a truly gifted internist, amazes me with her intelligence, judgment, and mastery.

It is also true that many of the Russians have not been able to find placement in their trained professions. It is sad, yet heartening, when we see a gentleman who looks more like a college professor sweeping the streets.

One of the highlights, living in Kiryat Arba, is the monthly concerts given by talented and highly competent Russian musicians. These well-attended, classical performances take place at the community center. Without fail, each is a masterpiece of perfection and beauty, worthy of huge concert halls. The Russians who attend are charming to watch. Sometimes as many as five of them bring large bouquets of fresh flowers, and present them to the maestros at the end of the concert. It is a token of the dignity and excellence which they brought with them to their new land, and which they preserve.

As I view the courage, endurance, and marvels of the people of Kiryat Arba, I ponder, "Am I worthy to be here beside them?" Viewing the surprises of my own life, I question, too, "What path have I taken which carried me from tranquil Utica, New York to this far-off, exotic place?"

I hope that the story of my own rocky road of bumps, tragedy, and serene gratification sheds some light for me and my readers.

CHAPTER TWO

They Called Me "Rainface"

The eye is not satisfied with seeing,
Nor the ear filled with hearing.
That which has been is that which shall be
And that which has been done
is that which shall be done;
And there is nothing new under the sun.

Ecclesiastes 1:3

As a psychologist, I see clearly how what I am today is the product of what I experienced as a child. I believe that my own school experiences, as a highly introspective child, provided a foundation for my career. In kindergarten and first grade I experienced a succession of events, including acute shyness, a month-long quarantine in the hospital, a brush with school phobia, and rescue by my mother from a potential reading disability. Each of these crises helped to lay the planks of sensitivity and wisdom which I would use later.

I learned early in my kindergarten year about the pains of shyness. Even though it was over fifty years ago, I still blush with shame when I remember those days. I longed to use a large climbing apparatus in the classroom, but was too self-conscious to try. I remember the agony of sitting in the kindergarten room watching the children play with this equipment, feeling too frightened to participate. Although I did eventually manage to have friends, the memory of watching the others play was a frustration which remains with me.

Adding to the imprisonment of abnormal shyness, in the spring of that kindergarten year an epidemic of scarlet fever broke out in my hometown, Utica, New York. Only five years of age when I was stricken with this highly contagious and dangerous illness, I became violently ill and had to be bed ridden. Since this took place before the advent of antibiotics, inoculations, and other "magic cures," there was no speedy recovery. There were signs on the doors of homes all over town warning that a patient, usually a child, was quarantined, and that it was dangerous to enter. I believe the front door to our home also posted such a sign. However, as I did have four older siblings, the doctor insisted that I be removed from the home and hospitalized, in order to guarantee their protection. The illness was so widespread that the large ward where I was placed had perhaps as many as twenty other children, all with scarlet fever.

As all of my siblings were by that time teenagers, I had a special role as the baby of the family, protected and fussed over by all. Naturally, the entire family was devastated by the trauma of my leaving home. They were all so thoughtful, trying to divert me when the ambulance drivers came to carry me off. They cushioned my departure by telling me about the new lilac bush that my father had planted on the front lawn. I was told repeatedly, "Thelma, look at the lilac bush when they carry you off the front porch." Of course, I was too overwhelmed and frightened, and forgot to look.

Although the first few days in the hospital passed in semi-delirium, my first recollection after that was of the flow of never-ending tears. These did not go unnoticed, especially by an older girl probably about age ten, whose bed was at the opposite end of the ward. When she dubbed me "Rainface," the name spread quickly. In my mind she was the meanest girl in the world.

The support of my family remained overflowing, however. My mother walked a considerable distance each day – as she had no auto – and then had to climb a ladder to reach the outside of the window near my bed, where she could talk to me. One day my fourteen-year-old brother, Manny, rode up to the window on his bicycle, and to my happy surprise, I saw an adorable new puppy in his basket.

I still remember one Friday afternoon, when my mother brought me two of my favorite dishes, chicken soup with noodles and lemon pie. I heard the nurse say "Yes" to the soup, but "No" to the pie. The thought of the two food items, which came from my parents' kosher, Jewish, Sabbath-observing home, immediately warmed my heart. The comfort and security which the Sabbath provided passed through me. I know now that the fact that there was no Kosher food available in hospitals in those days had to have been painful for my parents. Yet, they had no choice but to take life-saving measures in order to preserve my safety.

Unfortunately, it was common that some of these stricken children did not survive, and that many were left with heart defects. It wasn't until some time later that it was realized that there was some nerve damage to my ears, leaving me with a mild hearing loss. Fortunately the loss was mild enough that it did not require any treatment or interfere with schooling in any significant way.

After a month I was well again and was returned home to a grand reunion with my family. The biggest problem was that I refused to go back to my kindergarten class. After some days, as I played in front of my house, a friend called to me, "Thelma, here comes your teacher, Miss Sanford!" Yes, Miss Sanford was paying a home visit to my mother to discuss my prolonged absence. Because she had been the kindergarten teacher for all my siblings, she and my mother were old friends. She had no car and we had no phone, so she traveled by foot to our house.

Upon seeing her in the distance, I immediately ran into the yard and hid behind the garage. I stayed there until my friend reassured me "Yes, Miss Sanford is gone!" Finally believing that I was safe and that my kindergarten teacher had departed, I ran up the back stairs of our house to ask what had happened. I was relieved with my mother's comforting words, "Thelma, you won't have to return to kindergarten now, because it is already May, and so close to the end of the year. We can wait until September, when you will begin first grade."

Fortunately, Miss Sanford and my mother made a wise decision. They guessed that I would surely forget my fears over the summer, and that was exactly the way it happened. I was to learn much later, when treating school phobia cases during my own career, that they are not always that easy to remedy.

The next crucial event in my early schooling took place in the First Grade. I had a little girlfriend, Gladys, who was in my class as a first grade repeater. She observed that I was placed into the 'C' reading group, the lowest. While playing in my home a few days later, she announced to my mother, "Thelma is in the 'C' reading group. None of the children in that group get promoted, and must repeat first grade."

The very next day, my mother appeared at the classroom after school, for a conference with Miss Glancy, our first grade teacher. I even remember where they remained standing near the windows during a quite brief conference. Although I was asked to move to another part of the classroom, I could hear the conversation well.

My mother's plea to Miss Glancy was, "As you know, all of my older children are very good students. I'm certain that Thelma is as capable as they are. However, she is very shy. Perhaps if she receives a little more attention, she will do better."

Miss Glancy reacted quickly and positively. "I will be happy to give you a copy of the reader for use at home. If you have an adult member of the family practice with her, that may be helpful. Also, now that I know more about Thelma, I will certainly offer more support in the classroom."

As I listened intently, I was uplifted that my mother spoke with such confidence of my ability.

My thirteen-year-old sister, the next in age to me in the family, was assigned the task of helping me read at home. Books were not usually taken out of the classroom, and it was a battered and torn reader which the teacher had entrusted to us. Yet, for some reason I grew to love that book, and within a brief time I was moved to the 'B' reading group, and then to the 'A' group.

In my later work as a school psychologist, I always made a special note to repeat to parents the story of my mother's rescue. One important feature which I always included was that my mother – who had lived in a very small town, Kingston, New York, located on the Hudson River – had to leave school to work in a garment factory at the tender age of ten. Her own father died, and as the oldest child in the family, her wages were necessary. Yet, even with her limited schooling, she was able to avert the frustrations of life-long reading problems for her own child. "And you can, too," I encouraged the parents, "no matter what your background!"

During the middle of the third grade we moved, and I was placed in another neighborhood school. The first day, my mother took me to the class and introduced me to the teacher, Miss Cunningham, and stayed to observe. She was careful that I would not be too frightened in a new school. The teacher welcomed me warmly, and then gave me a page of math problems to complete, as a test of my ability. Since math was my strength, I breezed through the page. Miss Cunningham praised me highly for my accuracy and speed, so I was happy to be there. From then on, my elementary school days were charmed, and I was always recognized as one of the best in the class. My new school provided a great social situation as well, since half the class lived in my new neighborhood, and even attended the same afternoon Hebrew school as I did.

Many of these children became my best friends, with whom I still remain in touch.

At age fourteen when I entered high school, I was to experience a great shock. It was the only public high school in Utica, a city of one hundred thousand residents, and for me, it was much too large, competitive, and overwhelming. My school days were no longer charmed, since I had to work hard to maintain the grades to which I had been accustomed. Also, I no longer had the social crutch and familiarity of my old friends, and my shyness arose again. Even now it is embarrassing to remember that I stayed home one day to avoid taking my turn in public speaking in English class.

There were other things which were difficult for me. There was no college in Utica in those days, and no likelihood that my family would agree to college at all. All of the teachers my mother had known had never married, and my mother feared if I attended college, I would become a school teacher and a spinster, too. Thus, I was enrolled in the high school commercial track, in order to make me employable. Bored with some of these subjects, I felt cheated, and envied the students who were studying geometry and Latin.

My high school years took place during the Second World War, when every business was suffering from a shortage of workers. Thus, at the age of fourteen, much to my excitement and pleasure, my brother-in-law invited me to work in his large food market after school and on weekends, as a general clerk, cashier, and office worker.

I loved every minute of the atmosphere, the people, and being a part of the adult world. It kept me busy, since I spent much time on my homework late into the evenings. When I pushed myself hard, my mother would scold, "Thelma, you have spent enough time on your homework, please put your books away!"

My high school days were so filled that once, upon seeing a woman knitting on her porch, I remember thinking "How nice to have nothing to do but knit!" Little did I realize that many of the days of my life would be so filled, and that I would rarely find time to knit.

There was another part of me, though, brewing, in those high school days. I loved to read and pored through the novels of Charles Dickens, Jane Austin, and Charlotte and Emily Bronte. I was fascinated by the skills and wisdom of these authors, and their ability to describe and analyze the personalities, temperaments, and behaviors of their characters. In those days I began to realize, too, that friends seemed to enjoy confiding in me. In fact, one friend who was seeing a psychiatrist told me that she derived more comfort from telling her problems to me than to her therapist.

Thus, when I graduated from high school, I had fantasies of how gratifying it would be to help people with serious emotional problems, as a wise counselor. The study of psychology was uppermost in my mind. However, while at the public library searching for a book on careers,

I was shocked when I finally found just what I was looking for, a sort of job description for psychologists. It emphasized that most communities frequently call upon psychologists to serve as *public speakers*. Inasmuch as college was out of the question at that time, I consoled myself with the thought that I was too shy to speak publicly, anyway. It was that event in the library which shelved and postponed my fantasy of myself as a savior for others. Instead, after high school I took a position in a one-girl office, at a place I found dismal.

There was an excellent art school at the Manson Williams Proctor Institute in Utica, however. I always enjoyed drawing, so I enrolled in their evening program. Those three long evenings each week were a joy, the instructors and classmates inspirational and fun. Nevertheless, after one year of oil painting and another with clay, I learned little other than art theory. Even though I sketch well, I have no color sense, cannot paint, and my canvases and clay works were abysmal.

After a couple of years my friends began marrying. By that time I had begun to follow the path of my older siblings and that of virtually all the young people of Utica: Sabbath observance was dropped. Yet, I knew that I could not hurt my parents by dating the non-Jewish men who were so much more available than those who were Jewish. Thus, with a limited social life, I felt that life was passing me by. A new panic – "Perhaps there is no one in Utica for me to marry!" – pushed me into a drastic decision: to move to New York City.

It was not easy to persuade both my mother and father that I had to do this, since I was their youngest and in their eyes, would always be the "baby." But fortunately an aunt convinced them that I was of an age where I had to make my own decisions.

The day that I took the four-hour train ride to New York, embarking on my new adventure, my mother wept so much that she could not see me off at the station. Yet, alongside my anxiety over deserting her, was my anticipation for an exciting unknown venture! Even in my most hard-fisted skepticism concerning what I might expect on that four-hour train ride to New York, I awaited something. Perhaps at Grand Central Station more awaited me than I had any reason to expect....

CHAPTER THREE

New York City

Where men truly wish to go, their feet will manage to take them.

Talmud Tractate Succah 53a

As I sit here in Kiryat Arba, surrounded by the date palms and olive trees which adorn the front of our apartment building, it is so far away from the series of difficult experiences I endured while working as a bookkeeper in New York City. Nonetheless, I now see clearly how the sum total of those frustrating experiences fostered my calling to my totally gratifying career.

My first position was with the National Maritime Union. Thinking that unions were founded and motivated to champion the rights of all workers, I believed that I certainly would enjoy being there. However, as an accounts payable clerk, my desk was situated in a gigantic open room with many other clerks, all at their own desks. It gave me a feeling of insignificance and abandonment: I was a virtual cog in a wheel!

For what should have been a pleasant relief, there was a 15-minute coffee break each morning. But I found it difficult to return from the coffee break at the set moment, and, unknown to me, I was being carefully observed by the office manager. One day upon arriving from the break a couple of minutes late, he called me in to rebuke me, saying "Miss Alpert, you have not only overstayed your break, you also arrived at your desk this morning after nine o'clock."

Overwhelmed by feelings of imprisonment and humiliation, and naively confident that an abundance of positions were available, I immediately resigned.

After that experience, I searched for a position in a one-girl office, and found one immediately. It was a fabric converting business where three partners acted as middlemen for the process of dyeing raw fabrics into colors and designs. Although I remained there for many months, this office manager was also a source of stress for me. I was responsible for answering the phone, taking care of the correspondence, and also serving as a full-charge bookkeeper.

One surprising event did occur there, however. Each day it was my responsibility to phone a credit agency, where I spoke to the same young man. During the telephone friendship which developed, he often praised my "beautiful" speaking voice.

The compliment from this young man, whom I never saw, was a pleasant jolt to me. All of my life I had suffered from a mild articulation problem, having difficulty with the letter "s." In fact, in one of my first interviews for a position when I arrived in New York, I had been told, "No, we cannot hire you, you have a lisp, and what kind of impression would this make when you answered our phone?" Strangely, the lisp vanished that first year in New York, and she was the last person ever to mention it. This is something which I have never fully understood, but suspect somehow that growth in self-confidence played a role.

I found the office manager at the fabric converters to be a very disagreeable person. He would sometimes get quite upset treating with insensitivity what seemed like my small errors. I stayed there for many months, but finally left in a huff one day, feeling that his mean streak had gone too far. Before I left, one of the older partners, a kindly gentleman, tried, with no success, to change my mind: "Yes" he reassured me, "Mr. Gerber does have a temper. We try to overlook it, and we hope you will too, and that you'll stay with us." Nevertheless, as I now see from so many experiences which seemed so negative and pointless at the time, I probably gained skills and experience there which would be useful for my next position. Looking back, I know now that the "bosses" at the union and at the converter were doing their best, and that the real problem was that while I had much to learn, I truly hated this type of position.

My next try was another one-girl office, serving a lamp manufacturer. Here, I did the bookkeeping in a sort of solitary confinement. The owner was there most of the time, but spoke little.

On a rare occasion when the owner was out, however, a man appeared from nowhere! It seemed he was the foreman of the large lamp factory. Unknown to me, almost secretly, this factory was located just behind a door very near to the office. The foreman was a friendly man, and he was shocked when I told him, "I have never even been told that the factory is just behind that door." We both laughed as he took me through the factory and introduced me to the men who were assembling lamps.

Not too long later after this revelation my watch broke, but I kept neglecting to have it repaired. Each day in late afternoon, I would begin asking my employer the time, as I wanted desperately to know when it was 5:00 P.M., so that I could leave. Finally one day, he said to me, "Miss Alpert, what would happen if you worked a little overtime?" I thought to myself, "I'm so bored, I would quit!", and that was exactly what I did!

Despite my frustrations at each job, my social life flourished. It seemed everywhere I went there were available suitors who found me attractive. Gone were any feelings I may have had that my friends were prettier than I. However, there was a void of any religious content in my life, even though we bought only kosher food for the apartment which I shared with two girls.

By this time, after three different positions within just a year, I was quite discouraged about finding any pleasure working as a bookkeeper in the business world. But I had the good fortune to discuss my situation with a woman of much experience, a native New Yorker who was a successful office manager. She advised me that, rather than searching the want ads for a position, I should advertise my full-charge bookkeeping and secretarial skills in the classifieds, and then make a selection from the responses.

Little did I know that by following her advice I would enter a new world which would change my life.

As it turned out, strangely enough, I received only one response, from the accountant of a Jewish private school. His only child, a daughter, attended the school where he offered his professional services voluntarily. The school was at the Brooklyn Jewish Center, a Conservative synagogue located on Eastern Parkway in Brooklyn. It was an elementary school, serving students from kindergarten through eighth grade. Previously, a bookkeeper and a secretary performed the office duties, but in an effort to save money, their plan was to combine the two positions into one. After speaking with him on the phone, I learned that they would be thrilled to find someone with sufficient enthusiasm and naivete to take this on, and I was thrilled at the thought of leaving the world of commerce.

My first interview for the position was with Mrs. Anna Lesser, the principal. At that time I shared a modest apartment on Broadway, between 85th and 86th Street, with two girls. Since Mrs. Lesser lived nearby in a fine hotel on 86th Street, we agreed to meet at her apartment. I was startled when she told me that her building belonged to the estate of her late husband. The apartment was unforgettable: most of the floor space was crowded with beautiful, large pieces of furniture, all of which were saved from her most recent, more spacious home.

The interview was even more extraordinary than her apartment. A slender, tall, and dark haired woman, a natural beauty, she spoke non-stop about the school which employed her as principal and about the board of directors, which was made up of parents. She hinted that there were frictions between staff members of both the Hebrew and Secular departments, and there appeared to be a competition between them, with each upstaging the other. She told me that her academic degree had been in school psychology, and boasted proudly, "As principal of a modern religious day school, I am able to integrate the latest teaching methods."

She spoke on, at length, as though she were the interviewee, not I! Not one question was asked about my education, experience, or interests, and halfway through, I realized incredulously that without having spoken many words at all, I was already accepted for the position. Perhaps it was my quiet manner which appealed to her, or was it the fact that I was outfitted in my one and only well-coordinated business suit? The entire outfit gave me a "smart" look, although whenever I wore it, I felt like an imposter, fooling people about who I really was.

The Center Academy, the co-ed day school where I was to be employed, was located on the third floor of a magnificent, beautifully adorned Conservative synagogue building on Eastern Parkway. Also housed there were an afternoon Hebrew School, a banquet hall, a lending library, and even a swimming pool! It was explained to me that this concept of combining the synagogue with a community center was a new one sweeping the country. (Now, a half-century later, we can say the theory did not hold water.) I was elated at the opportunity to leave the business world, yet never dreamed that this position would eventually lead to three of the most important aspects of my life: my career, my move to Orthodox Judaism, and marriage to my brilliant and loving life-mate.

There were so many things to learn in this new position, and it was all overwhelming! It really was a position for two people, but I found everything so interesting, I arrived early, stayed late, and enjoyed every minute of it. I even stole time from my own lunch hour – true to form – to walk to the bank to deposit the tuition checks which I handled.

Gradually, over time, as I mastered the requirements of my position at the Center Academy, I began to realize the importance of the functions of a school secretary. Why, I was the key person who ran the school! In later years in my role as a school psychologist, I shared this little-known secret with many school secretaries. And all of them would readily agree, "Yes, the secretary really runs the school!"

What a contrast with the solitary confinement of the lamp factory office! Here, my desk was usually surrounded by teachers and students with all kinds of requests, or just to chat. Things were so busy there, it was often impossible to complete the business at hand. Mrs. Lesser, the overall principal, was particularly chatty, and her desk stood a few feet behind mine. Dr. Leo Shpall, the Hebrew principal who became a special friend, was also a frequent visitor at my desk. As these school heads were both in their 50s and I was in my early 20s, I found their professional confidence in me very flattering.

To be admitted to the Center Academy, students were required to be evaluated by a psychologist. This was quite advanced for the 50s, as school psychology was still in its infancy. Mrs. Lesser had engaged a former classmate to administer these intelligence tests outside of the school. The psychologist's reports were always late in coming, and in order to expedite matters, I was sometimes asked to type them. I read those which I typed with fascination, but even then, I thought the reports were rather skimpy. However, I loved the parts where behavioral observations were noted, and each time I read one, I would say to myself, "I could do that. I could do it better!" Little did I realize that "school psychology seeds" were being planted in my brain which were not to be germinated until many years later.

The religious philosophy of the Center Academy followed that of the Brooklyn Jewish Center, which was affiliated with the Conservative movement. Yet Dr. Shpall, the head of the Hebrew Department, along with all of his Hebrew teachers, were Orthodox Jews. Although I had grown up in such a home in Utica, my religious studies background was quite limited. Thus, I had followed the lead of all of my older siblings – and of the general trend of the entire younger generation of Jewish people in Utica – that religious observance was old fashioned and "not for today."

Exposure to Dr. Shpall and his staff, all practicing Orthodox Jews, had a profound effect on me. I began to realize that they had a rich quality in their lives which I did not share, and I began to envy them.

For example, walking a couple of blocks from the subway to the school one day, I was accompanied by Miss Feder, one of the Hebrew teachers, and Mr. Sussman, the science teacher. Mr. Sussman, a non-observant Jewish man, began to question Miss Feder about her religious practices.

"As a student of science myself, I am wondering how an educated person like you can follow orthodox beliefs, especially the Biblical miracles?" Her confident response, "I have faith!" had a profound effect on me. I found myself envious of her conviction, and felt a new awareness in myself. A dormant religious longing became evident.

I also began to realize that, although I knew that my ancestors of eons ago originated from Palestine, I had no idea why my more recent ancestors lived in Europe before migrating to Utica, New York.

In order to learn more, I decided to take a course in Jewish History at the New School for Social Research, located in Manhattan. Although the instructor was not a religiously observant man, he was well known as an outstanding scholar of Jewish history. His course turned out to provide the fountain of information which I was seeking, and helped me to begin to understand who I was.

Because of my meager exposure to history, each class, beginning from Biblical times to the present, was an awesome, shocking awakening! I began to learn of the three thousand years of religious and intellectual gifts of the Jews to the world, and of the strife which they had to endure in order to survive. Realizing the miracle of each Jewish survivor who lives today played a role in moving me to embrace a life of Jewish observance.

In my three-and-a-half years at the Center Academy, the staff members with whom I became closest were all males. Chiefly it was because they were less confined to the classroom than most of the female teachers, and had more time to chat around my desk. Besides Dr. Shpall, Lou Harris, the art teacher, and David Weintraub, the music teacher, became my special friends.

One day Mrs. Lesser asked Mr. Harris, whom she knew was divorced and lived alone in Greenwich Village, "Do you eat your meals at home or at restaurants?"

His response – "I only go to restaurants when I can afford it!" – seemed to startle her. Determined to help this struggling artist, she had a brainstorm that he could earn extra money by doing pastel drawings of the students. To serve as a sample for the parents to see, he did one of me, and it hung on the school office wall behind Mrs. Lesser's desk. To this day, I treasure it highly, and it hangs in a prominent place in my living room in Kiryat Arba.

My other friend, David Weintraub, was a talented classical pianist with a magnificent cantorial voice, whose father was Rabbi at an orthodox synagogue in Philadelphia. As we became better acquainted, he began telling me of a wonderful young man, Arnold Blumberg, who had already earned his Ph.D. in History from the University of Pennsylvania, and who was president of his father's synagogue. However, it seemed Arnold was not too enthusiastic about traveling to New York to meet me, and wanted to see a photo first. I already had a busy social life, and I found the idea of a photo appalling, so I refused. However, David persisted for many months, until he persuaded us to meet. When Arnold arrived at the door for our first date, his first words were, "A pretty picture, and a pretty girl!"

Arnold and I were married six months after we met, and I left the Center Academy for the suburbs of Philadelphia, where we established our Sabbath-observant home. When I left the Brooklyn Jewish Center all of my loving friends gave me a memorable and generous farewell.

David, who went on to earn his Ph.D in music, remains our friend to this day, and now lives in Ramat Gan, Israel, with his wife and children. We have always marveled that he had the foresight to see that Arnold and I were soul mates, and that he put such a huge effort into bringing us together.

When I left the Center Academy, as in so many of my life's experiences, I did not realize the full extent of what I had gained there. In addition to meeting my precious husband, and guidance toward religious observance, the seeds of my calling were planted.

CHAPTER FOUR

Michael

*" . . As you travel through this world you will
see much that will strike you as unjust.... But
understand that G-d works in mysterious ways."*
Elijah the Prophet in The Classic Tales: 4,000
Years of Jewish Lore by Ellen Frankel

Our son Raphael and our daughter Eva were born in Philadelphia, where we lived for three-and-a-half years. At the birth of each perfect, beautiful child, we marveled at the miracle of it all, and there was no more contented family and appreciative parents than we.

We were thrilled when we moved our little family to Baltimore where my husband, a history professor, accepted a position at Towson State College. Life seemed so complete. To add to our joy, after one year in Baltimore, our youngest child, Michael, was born, in 1959.

I gave little thought at the time of Michael's birth that it took many, many hours for the anesthesia to wear off, and for the nurses to awaken me. In those days less consideration was given to the fact that an overdose could be harmful to a newborn. But, even after I awakened, Michael too was such a sleepy, groggy newborn that we had to wait many more hours before he was presented to us. He was an eight-and-a-half pound, physically well-developed, beautiful baby, and in our minds, we were truly blessed in every way with our remarkable family. We never dreamed then that my sleepiness and the baby's was the probable result of an overdose of anesthesia, which would turn out to have a profound effect on the baby.

When I took Michael home I gave little thought that he was a very slow feeder, and that his developmental milestones during the first year were much delayed. We always found some reasonable excuses that he did not sit, stand, walk, or feed himself as early as our other children. After all, we comforted ourselves, he eventually did learn to perform all of these gross motor tasks. If any doubts about his development ever crossed my mind as I lay in bed at night, they would be quickly dispelled in the morning, when I saw this beautiful smiling child standing in his crib, wearing what appeared as a charming, intelligent expression. What I did not realize then was that at the same time he bore such an intelligent and handsome countenance, there was absolutely no eye contact.

About that time I read a biography of Albert Einstein and was pleased when I learned that he, too, developed slowly when he was a pre-schooler. I derived comfort from telling myself that Michael had some remarkably brilliant ancestors, and that his superior intelligence would surely be proven. Many years later, in my work as a school psychologist, I was startled by a comment made by another mother while we were discussing her intellectually challenged child. Her words, echoing mine, were: "I didn't worry about my child's delays; I had read that Einstein also appeared delayed when he was a toddler."

However, when Michael passed age two-and-a-half, and still spoke no words, we did begin to panic. It all came into focus one day while my husband and I were relaxing in a park with the children. Playfully, I asked my six-year-old son, Raphael, "If you could be granted any wish, what would you wish for most?"

I was shocked when he responded, "I would want Michael to speak!" Suddenly, I was struck by the gravity of the situation. The thought that this was the uppermost longing of my oldest child, not yet a first grader, disconcerted me.

Belatedly, I know about the multi-disciplinary and well- coordinated evaluations and services offered today for disabled pre-schoolers. I realize now that Michael was born more than a generation too soon! In the early 1960s the evaluation process was rather hit-or-miss, and this contributed to a six-month period of excruciating emotional pain while Michael was being seen by a series of professionals.

I began my search for answers by having Michael seen first at the then-famous Harriet Lane Speech Clinic at Johns Hopkins Hospital (a service that no longer exists there). The clinician there who saw Michael treated me brutally, or at least it seemed so. Of course, she had no inkling that I believed I had a little boy, nearly age three, who was of above-average intelligence, and whose only problem was delayed speech. Instead, after she attempted to evaluate him, her shrill words to me were, "I can't evaluate him! His problems are too severe! He's either emotionally disturbed or mentally retarded." It was one of the cruelest, most shocking days of my life. When I returned home, it was difficult to explain to my husband what I had been through. The tears just began to flow.

Next, my pediatrician made an appointment for Michael with Dr. Leon Eisenberg, a child psychiatrist who was also at Johns Hopkins Hospital. He was well known as a key figure connected with Dr. Leo Kanner, famous for identifying autism. Together, they were responsible for establishing a special program for preschoolers with emotional problems at the Children's Guild.

By that time, I had fantasies of Michael being placed there and attaining normalcy before first grade. But, Dr. Eisenberg's services were in such demand, that our appointment was delayed for four months! The agony of waiting was indescribable, as the most elementary of words, such as "Da Da" or "Momma," escaped Michael. Yet, when the day of the appointment finally arrived, my husband and I were totally unprepared for the results. At worst, I worried that the little boy had some kind of learning problem. This alone would certainly have been a disaster for us, in terms of the dreams parents have for their children. Dr. Eisenberg, as a psychiatrist, had a young staff psychologist take Michael into another room for the evaluation. By this time, after all the delays, Michael was already three-and-a half. The psychologist returned with Michael quite quickly, presenting her results to the doctor, who quietly informed us that the diagnosis was "profound mental retardation." I feel now that he tried to present this in a gentle manner, but his words, "The best Michael might ever achieve in life would be to deliver packages," were tantamount to a death sentence.

What we did not realize at that moment was that his prediction of "best" was far above reality.

When we reported to our pediatrician, he told us to request these results in a written report. Neither in writing or by phone was this report ever received. In view of Michael's handsome and intelligent countenance, our pediatrician, too, did not believe he could have been as disabled as had been described by Dr. Eisenberg's psychologist. Thus, he then made other appointments: with Dr. Glazer, the most important child psychiatrist at the University of Maryland, and with a well-known neurologist, as well. However, they too confirmed the diagnosis.

The day we left Dr. Eisenberg's office, the tears began to flow, non-stop, for days that ran into months. I knew then that when a child is lost through illness and death, G-d forbid, there is a mourning period and life goes on. But for us there was no mourning period, nor any programs, training, or remediation for Michael. In the depth of my despair, I truly did not wish to live.

The only service recommended was through parent meetings of the Baltimore Association for Retarded Citizens (BARC). When I first called for an appointment, sobbing into the phone, I could not get through the conversation. I had to hang up, collect myself, and call back. I went to the first meeting by myself. My husband was not ready to admit to himself or to the world that Michael was retarded, or "challenged," as they now say. However, I did find some comfort from meeting other parents, from sharing tales of horror about the cruel professionals out there, and the dearth of any kind of service for our disabled children. Another small source of comfort came from a social worker from BARC, who made a home visit. After viewing Michael's good looks, it was consoling to hear her say, "When a child is normal in appearance, but functions within the profound range, the parental adjustment is more difficult."

After many months of hearing about my despair, my pediatrician suggested I see a psychiatrist. I was appalled at his idea, since I knew, rightly, that what I really needed was some help for Michael. In the 1960s there were no special pre-school programs – no speech therapy, occupational therapy, or physical therapy – none of the services which today enrich the lives of disabled pre-schoolers of all levels. No, we were doubly damned, first by the prolonged evaluation process, and then by the fact that there were just no services for our handicapped child.

Our experiences, multiplied by thousands of such family tragedies, represent another sad phase in the evolution of services for the intellectually impaired, from the days of the "idiot" label to that of the "developmentally disabled." Yet, as a school psychologist, looking back, I am amazed at the great strides which have taken place in both evaluations and services, in the past two generations.

An unexpected turn in Michael's life occurred when he was five-years-old. On a one-day visit to Philadelphia, my husband's hometown, he spoke of Michael's problems to a cousin, a take-charge, career supervisor of nurses at a large hospital. She told him of a new program in Philadelphia for children with problems such as Michael's, called the "Institutes for the Development of Human Potential." It was rumored that they were able to work wonders, stimulating and improving the intellectual development of young children like ours. It was the first glimmer of any kind of treatment, and we became euphoric with hope.

Michael

Our first diagnostic appointment was just preceding the Labor Day holiday in 1964, and we were told to be prepared to spend two entire days there. We took our older children along, and all of us were guests of kind friends. While our hosts entertained and babysat the older children, we spent two days at the Institutes.

The grounds and converted mansions of the Institutes were located on Stenton Avenue. The expanse of which they occupied and the magnificence of the buildings alone built up our hopes even more.

Accounts of the Institutes were spreading. Desperate parents from all parts of the country, all with children similar to Michael, were seeking appointments. On each day they evaluated as many as 35 children. As we sat in the waiting room, I saw some children there who were as handsome and normal appearing as Michael, while also just as tragically limited, noisy, and hyperactive.

I was fascinated that their method for evaluation of children – all delayed in multiple ways and with no language skills – was based primarily on sensory responses. They did not measure a child's visual-motor and verbal skills in the traditional manner, by comparing them to the norm. Instead, the level of development was measured via the basic processes which the child actually used to see, hear, and touch. It was theorized that brain injury interfered with all of these functions, and that by rejuvenating unused, healthy brain cells, intellectual growth would occur.

For the first time ever, the evaluation process for Michael seemed to make sense. There was no IQ level assigned to him, but rather, a profile of strengths and weaknesses of his sensory responses. The evaluation therapists were treating him as a human being with some hope for the future, rather than a being relegated to a scrap heap! However, we were told that we would not know until the end of the day whether Michael would be accepted for the program. Needless to say, we were extremely anxious.

At the end of the long day, our turn came for the decision regarding Michael's acceptance. We sat nervously at the conference, waiting to hear the words, "Yes, we feel Michael is one of our candidates whom we may be able to help" and we bubbled with joy when, indeed, we finally heard them. We were told to arrive the next day at an early hour, to dress warmly, and to be prepared to remain very late in the evening. We had no inkling what the treatment involved, and were puzzled about the warm clothing.

The answers to our questions came the next day, which would turn out to be one of the most interesting days of our lives.

Upon arrival at the Institutes at eight in the morning with Michael, we were assigned to an auditorium with a group of about fifty other parents. Other arrangements were made for the care of the children. The reason for the warm clothing was obvious, soon after being seated. Although it was a balmy September day, the temperature in the room must have been no more than sixty degrees, geared to keep us alert for the four-hour lecture.

Glenn Doman, one of the founders of the Institutes, then proceeded to deliver a non-stop lecture for four hours! A well-trained, brilliant orator, and an experienced physical therapist, he focused on every facet of mental retardation. Of course, this was a topic which would surely arouse the emotions of these neglected-by-the-world parents, and he was as moving as a fire-and-brimstone preacher. His knowledge seemed infinite, as he detailed intricate historical accounts of physicians, neurologists, psychologists, psychiatrists, educators, and physical therapists in their "treatment," "non-treatment," or abuse of brain damaged children. And since each parent had his own tale of woe, even a less-gifted orator could have reached this audience.

He discussed intelligence, the brain, and how his own failures, experiments, and successes as a physical therapist led to his current role. Even more exciting, he kept referring to the fact that we, as parents, had the ability to improve and even cure our afflicted children. As we sat there, we still had no inkling of what he was actually speaking about, in terms of what we were going to be asked to do.

The major focus of the treatment was a practically overwhelming obligation of time and personal commitment required of each family. Then, the objectives of the lecture we had heard in that cold, cold room, all fell into place. There was no way that any family could think of following such a regimen without having been kept alert by cool air and by being prepared by Glenn Doman's passionate rhetoric. Indeed, we knew we had been brainwashed, and that the program which we were about to accept would require an almost intimidating level of commitment.

Our program consisted of four five-minute sessions of body movement, conducted by three people, who were to put Michael's body through the crawling movements, as he lay face down on a table. Although he was age five and could walk, all of Michael's waking moments were to be spent on his stomach on the floor, crawling and creeping. It would take a total of thirty-five volunteers to help with this "patterning," as the table exercises were called. It would take superhuman determination to follow through with a program which, on the surface, appeared as some kind of hocus pocus insanity.

As time went on and we proceeded to solicit volunteers and to keep Michael on the floor, we would understand more and more clearly each day, the purpose of the "brain washing" in that cold room.

My first "volunteer" was my next-door neighbor, a sweet, kindly woman, whom I practically dragged to my home to help. She kept declaring that she knew nothing about these things, and would not be able to help, but, when she saw the simple task assigned her, and that she was needed, she seemed pleased with herself. She remained a faithful volunteer for the next two-and-a-half years. My husband spoke to the president of our synagogue, Shearith Israel, asking if he could make an appeal for volunteers. Although the president appeared to decline the favor, he had a better idea. Very quietly he asked a nurse who belonged to our congregation to enlist volunteers. That remarkable woman not only built a corps of volunteers, but also created a schedule ensuring that they would come to our door within a carefully planned time. The Chevra Ahavas Chesed organization, made up of Jews who had survived Hitler's holocaust in Germany, also provided a very dependable corps of volunteers.

I was touched by the interest and compassion of all these people, most of whom were previously unknown to us, being new to the neighborhood and the synagogue. In fact, one neighbor who lived across the street knocked on our door one day, opening her conversation with "I know people are coming to help you with your son. I have no idea what you are doing, but even though I am seventy-three-years-old, I want to help also."

When Michael's problems first became evident, I did develop a bitterness when a couple of close friends, with whom I had been in daily contact, cut themselves off from us completely and stopped phoning. Yet, once these same people knew of some specific way to be helpful, they became loyal volunteers. It is a lesson which has remained with me – people often do want to help, but are simply ashamed over not knowing what to do.

The next six months were very exciting for us all. Michael showed faster growth in comprehension skills and motor development than in any period of his life. For example, initially, it was as though Michael could not hear, and whenever I called to him, it would be necessary to repeat his name loudly three times until his attention could be engaged. But, within some weeks, I would merely whisper his name, and he was at my side! The uncanny part was the speed with which he began to follow directions, that is, those within his limitations. One morning he would amaze me by putting his shirt over head, and on another, put on his sock, taking care that the heel was in place. And although before the program he went through an unprovoked tantrum at least once a week, during which he would scream and cry and lash out uncontrollably for at least one hour, these tantrums disappeared completely!

The most amazing feature was the reduction of his hyperactivity. Previously I had been feeding him salty pretzels to calm him down, resulting in much thirst and drinking. When we were told to eliminate all salty foods, and to limit his daily fluids to twenty ounces a day, the change was miraculous, even before we began the exercises.

The Institutes were far advanced in the early treatment of children who experience delays. Since then, I have had many opportunities to observe the progress achieved by physical, occupational, and speech therapists, treating children right from birth, using many of the very activities which the Institutes promoted. At the time, traditional medicine criticized them unfairly and accused them of taking advantage of a vulnerable population. I believe however, that their only fault was the promise to parents that their children would be cured, rather than significantly helped.

In Michael's case, despite a number of activities concentrated on speech development, sadly there was no progress. Most of the gains were made during the first six months, but because we were so elated and encouraged by this progress, and spurred on by our volunteers, we were reluctant to discontinue. Every two months we were scheduled for re-evaluation, but by the end of two-and-a half years, we all knew it was time to move on to other things.

The volunteers proved to play an interesting and important role in our lives. In the beginning, each time someone arrived, I was able to relate Michael's progress of the week. It became a satisfaction and motivation for them to continue as well as for us. Some of these people would be chronically late, and others so prompt that they would arrive five minutes early and wait in their cars until the designated time, so as not to disturb us. As I became better acquainted with their habits, I began to switch schedules around for more compatibility. Many enjoyed the visit with us, and stayed on to talk, and remain among our best friends till today.

Michael

In terms of my own mental health, this program was certainly the best thing which could have happened. The exposure to all of these volunteers paved the way for me to serve as a speaker and advisor at parent groups. Furthermore, while previously I had desisted from telling occasional friends about our son, because their comments upset me; I now held back because I didn't want to upset them.

As Michael grew into his teen years, it became more and more difficult for the family to manage his care. Perhaps the most painful life decision we ever made was to place him in residential care. However, I feel that due to the program of the Institutes, we were able to enhance his limited skills, and to keep him in our home with us for a much longer period. He now receives outstanding care at the Rosewood Center in Baltimore, an excellent state facility.

When Michael was very young I set two goals for our family. First of all, I determined to do everything in my power to care for Michael's special needs. Secondly, I determined that I would not let his handicaps interfere with the intellectual or social growth of any other members of our family. I feel we succeeded in fulfilling our goals. Our son and our daughter have successful careers and beautiful families. They have presented us with ten wonderful grandchildren. My husband was able to publish six books in the area of his specialty, diplomatic history. Later, I finished graduate school and entered my career in school psychology. It is always heartwarming when a younger friend or acquaintance who has faced some adversity tells me, "I watched what you did, and you were my inspiration to pursue my career!"

Yet there are two factors over which I will never have control. The first of these, which is of lesser importance and difficult to admit, is that to this day I am extremely uncomfortable with the stares of strangers when taking Michael anywhere in public. Although he is now a young man, he continues to attract the attention of strangers, particularly children. I would have no problem accepting the stares for myself, but I find it intolerable for my son.

The second factor, which is of greatest importance, is his inability to communicate the location of any physical pain which he feels, either with speech or pointing. To me this is the cruelest affliction of all for any human being, and, it creates feelings of helplessness too torturous for any mother!

At the same time, I am keenly aware that there has been a distinct psychological and spiritual enrichment to the lives of all my family members. Some time ago, I read of a Korean War veteran who had been imprisoned and tortured over a prolonged period. He related that the experience had elevated him to a higher level of understanding life, creation, and G-d. It is easy for me to identify with these thoughts. I know that my own growth in wisdom, resulting from Michael's handicaps, is almost indescribable.

My original concerns that our child would always carry the label of the "intellectual limited," seems now so shallow. Our concerns are now more mature and realistic, as we view him as physically and neurologically damaged.

About the time that we learned of Michael's problems, a friend lost her husband of only ten years. Her comment to me was, "Oh, what happened to you is so much worse!" I wondered then how she could measure and compare grief, and since then I have repeated to others: "There is no real measure for grief."

Most people assume that I chose school psychology as my life work because of my experiences with Michael. I have repeated again and again, that it is not so. What is very true is that it has enhanced every aspect of my work, in my treatment of children with problems, their parents, and their teachers.

PHASE TWO
Agonies and Ecstasies

CHAPTER FIVE

Brief Encounters Cement the Path

The wise man is he who can learn from every man.
Sayings of the Fathers 4:1

When we ended our intense program with Michael, who was then seven-years-old, five successive events in my life shaped my direction firmly into a career as an inner-city school psychologist. As with many key events in life, the first two came about in an unexpected way that was unrelated to psychology. They took place when we enrolled Michael in a private program for intellectually limited children. At that time there was no law for schooling the severely and profoundly mentally retarded. Nevertheless, there was a small private program available under the auspices of the Baltimore Association of Retarded Children. The school was located on Denmore Avenue, in Baltimore, in a single-floor, wood-frame, run-down structure. It housed a central hall and two large classrooms, one on either side. The teacher, Mrs. Toni Bernstein, was excellent though, and we were thrilled with the instruction and attention that Michael received.

I once asked about the origin of this small, strange building where Michael's school was located. It disturbed me to learn that the two room structure had been the segregated elementary school for non-white children, before the advent of integration. Having grown up in New York State, this was my first exposure to segregated schools. I was horrified, because I knew that just two blocks away, on Rogers Avenue, stood a large, beautiful old brick school building, Arlington Elementary.

I couldn't help but be reminded at this time of an incident which took place in my home when I was a teenager. My father, who was a shoemaker by trade, was a highly affable and intelligent man. People of all walks of life enjoyed sitting and talking to him while he worked. One day as we ate dinner at home, he told us about a new friend. It seems he was an African-

American man whom he described as a well-read, scholarly gentleman. He then told us, "And do you know where he works? He cleans the toilets of the city jail." As he said this, tears rolled down his cheeks. These memories of my father and his friend, along with the dilapidated segregated school building, were to remain with me, and they served as a cornerstone of my thoughts during the years when I served as a school psychologist at the inner city schools.

The next of these chance events began when Michael was picked up each day by a yellow school bus. Seated on his bus were a variety of handicapped children from many different programs located throughout the city. High body motion and constant rocking were common to many of the bus passengers, and they attracted attention easily when the bus stopped.

Thus, one day as the bus was parked in front of my house waiting for Michael, a short, plump middle-aged couple was passing by. I was amazed that they stopped in their tracks at the edge of our property and stood there staring at the children. Their staring angered me, and remained with me until I had a surprise meeting with one of them some time later. On that occasion I had been assigned to do some work with a group of emotionally and intellectually impaired adults at the Jewish Community Center. To my surprise, on the very first day, I saw sitting in the group the short plump lady who stood on the street staring at my son. This was an excellent example for me about how easy it is to waste energy when we misperceive the actions of others.

I was to utilize this insight throughout my career with middle school students and their teachers. Some of the most disruptive teenagers with whom I worked would pick fights with peers when just accidentally touched or bumped in the crowded halls. Similarly, some teachers would develop distorted views of the motives of some of their unruly students, often mistaking fear for malice. Thus, my simple words declaring to both the teachers and students that "Things are rarely the way they seem!"paved the way for mending many conflicts.

With Michael now settled in a school program, and with my older children already in fifth and seventh grades, I began to fantasize being employed once again. I knew that I no longer wished to work as a bookkeeper, and so it was then that my life-long dream of earning a college degree became a reality. I had no clear career choice as I entered college, but three additional events clarified my path.

Brief Encounters Cement the Path

My ultimate goal was to enroll at Towson University, then called Towson State College, where my husband taught. However, I wished to avoid any required history classes with professors who were colleagues or personal friends of my husband. Thus, I enrolled at the Community College of Baltimore for two years, taking the required history courses there. Another requisite - and one which I still dreaded - was that of a public speaking course.

As it turned out, the instructor in public speaking wisely required each student to deliver a talk each week, beginning from week one of the semester. Although I had the advantage of being twenty years older than some of the other students, my chronic shyness and fear of speaking publicly were so much in evidence that I began to think of ways to overcome it. For example, I once heard that imagining that people in the audience were wearing no clothing would help, and I even considered that.

However, the instructor and the simple text book which he assigned were excellent, and I gradually learned to deliver a fairly good speech. After each session he gave the students an opportunity to comment to the class on the talks of their classmates. I was amazed one day when one young girl volunteered, "Thelma's talks are so great! I could listen to her all day." It was this remark, combined with the repeated talks which I was forced to present, which ignited a spark. A foundation was laid for me to become a desired speaker, a useful skill in my later career.

So from this unexpected direction, facing my greatest fear, as it were, my career path was greatly cleared. Now, whenever I hear anyone say "Please do not call on me to speak, I am not a speaker!" I am reminded of my educated conviction, "Most anyone can learn to speak publicly!"

When I entered Towson State for my Junior and Senior year, I selected Psychology as a major, and after earning my Bachelor's degree, I was elated when I entered Towson's excellent master's program in Psychology. It was as though I had been waiting all of my life to study the Rorschach and the Thematic Apperception tests, measures of personality, along with the tests of intelligence. I was ecstatic to be exploring the secrets of the minds of human beings. Doors were now open to me for more knowledge, all of which I equated, in a religious sense, to minute seeds for understanding life. Without a doubt, this phase of my schooling was among my life's most significant milestones.

We began by using theoretical cases, and then moved on to real people. We were required to find twenty of our own subjects, both children and adults, with whom to administer these evaluations. As I began to line up my candidates, I was delighted to find neighbors and friends who would volunteer their children and themselves as "guinea pigs" for my apprentice testing. During those days, my husband used to joke, "You are the only psychologist I know who makes home visits!"

Although the course work and the field experience combined were demanding and exhausting, I found all of this fascinating and gratifying. I feel special indebtedness to my superb professors, Dr. Barbara Slater and Dr. Stanley Zweback.

Yet then, we reached a point in the program where I had to make a choice – I could continue in either of two programs: School Psychology or Clinical Psychology. That semester I learned belatedly that in order to qualify for working with adults, I needed one year of clinical counseling. Believing that I could only succeed with adults, I felt devastated when I learned that I was in the behavior management tract, and that my degree would qualify me for working only with children. I immediately went to the professor assigned to the counseling program, pleading for entrance. He firmly rejected my plea, saying the class was full, and to this day, I credit him with forcing me onto the path which I took, that of working with my beloved young students.

The final milestone event which shaped the direction of my career proved to be a behavior management class. It was my very first exposure to the idea that, by our own behavior, we can significantly affect the behavior of others. As I read the overly simplified texts we studied, I was filled with amazement and disbelief. On the other hand, the major class term paper required that we each work with a live subject outside of class, to demonstrate what we had learned. I was very busy at the time with my own teenagers and three different car pools, to say nothing of my other course work, and wondered how I would find time to concentrate on such an involved project.

Luckily I found an easy way out, and was able to select a cousin and her fifteen-year-old daughter, who lived right around the corner from our house.

In the mind of my cousin, she and her daughter didn't have a serious problem. She felt we were stretching the point when we concentrated on one simple behavior, that of her daughter's failure to return any object to its place either in her room or around the house. And, as my cousin knew that her daughter would not agree to this project, we could only do this without her knowledge. Her daughter was a productive teenager who was artistically inclined, and who enjoyed baby-sitting for many hours with pre-school children. Among her talents were stringing necklaces, drawing, painting, crafts, and sewing. Her scotch tape, markers, crayons, scissors, threads, etc., would be messily strewn all around the house. Regardless of how much her mother nagged and scolded, she never could persuade her to put any of her materials away, and of course it isn't unusual that mothers and daughters of this age sometimes do not "operate together" smoothly.

My cousin was certain that she could not discuss this project with her daughter, so we proceeded in another manner. Basically, I concentrated on changing my cousin's own behavior. My plan was for her to ignore totally any materials left around her room and the house, and to praise her daughter when she did put anything in it's place. The results, when the mother changed her own behavior, were astonishing.

One day when the teenage daughter returned the postage stamps to the stationery drawer and her mother said, "Thank you for returning the stamps," there was total silence and a look of amazement on the girl's face. On another occasion, when the daughter was praised for putting orange juice back in the refrigerator, she replied, "I didn't put it back, I finished it." Either she felt she didn't deserve the praise, or perhaps she was becoming suspicious about what was happening.

Nevertheless, the girl's language and manner towards her mother changed dramatically. For example, she surprised her one day by calling out as she was at the front door ready to leave, "Mom, is there anything I can get you at the store?" I was astonished and elated when my cousin later told me, "I can't believe my daughter's behavior has changed so drastically! It's a real miracle!"

My success with this simple project has proven to be a foundation for my later work with children. It is a topic which I have studied more extensively, lectured about to parents and teachers, and published articles. It proved to be a cornerstone for success with improving children's behavior, one which I have enjoyed throughout my career.

Following completion of my courses came my next challenge, a full year of internship in School Psychology. Thanks to the excellent Master's program at Towson State, along with unforeseen milestone events, the die was cast for my career, and I was better prepared than I realized for the next phase....

CHAPTER SIX

Internship in Jerusalem

*For want of counselors a people will fall; but
safety lies in a wealth of counselors.*
Book of Proverbs 11:14

Our apartment in Kiryat Arba is about an hour bus ride from Jerusalem. These days the buses are bullet proof in order to offer protection, due to the Arab *Intifada*. Nevertheless, it is always a comfortable, scenic ride through the mountains to Jerusalem. As we wind along the mountain road, I sometimes enjoy pleasant memories of a time some years ago, when we spent six months in Jerusalem.

In the fall of 1975, I was to enjoy a one-semester internship, otherwise known as the "crowning fulfillment" of knowledge learned in graduate school. As it happened, that was the same semester when my husband had a sabbatical, planning to spend six months doing research in Israel. By that time Michael was relatively comfortable in his private residential school in Delaware, and our two older children were in college-based programs in Israel, Michlala and Yeshiva Kerem B'Yavna.

To my astonishment, I succeeded in locating an internship placement in Jerusalem. Each step of planning posed obstacles which appeared insurmountable. It took hours of time and effort, while still in Baltimore, merely to locate a suitable school for English-speaking youngsters, gain the approval of the Psychology Department, and to assemble the numerous evaluation and counseling materials. I then had to make the difficult decision as to which of my precious notes and reference books to take in the very limited space allowance.

Miraculously, I found myself in Jerusalem in August of 1975, ready to tackle the unknown. We were fortunate to find a large furnished apartment in the Rechavia neighborhood, with its beautiful stone-fenced gardens.

The school of my choice was the Summit Institute, a residential facility for emotionally handicapped adolescents. American parents had sent their youngsters to this treatment center in Israel after all other options had failed them. The students, faculty, and therapeutic staff were largely English-speaking, but other unanticipated obstacles appeared upon my arrival in Jerusalem.

At the top of the list of new obstacles was my own full-blown case of culture shock. Housekeeping in our furnished apartment – which used bottled gas – and shopping for and using Israeli groceries, all required adjustment. For instance, one day my husband asked, "Why do you have the cooking oil and the bleach next to each other on the kitchen counter?" What he thought was bleach was really vinegar, easily confused, since the bottles are identical. As difficult as learning about traveling on buses seemed, after some weeks I was surprised to find myself helping others. In addition, at that time the school, which had recently relocated, did not yet have a phone, a common circumstance back in 1975. It took great persistence merely to locate the director and to find the school.

Secondly, the director suddenly had doubts about the need for my services, which appeared to him to be largely diagnostic. He argued that the Summit Institute's total emphasis was therapeutic, rather than diagnostic, and that schedules were all filled. He feared that these intelligent students, who had been exposed to testing much of their lives, would laugh and ridicule my efforts. Nonetheless, he did invite me to a meeting at the school, and said that if I could convince the students that they needed me, I could stay on.

That first meeting proved to be an anxious one, since their reactions to me were lukewarm to cool. I was certain I would be rejected when one student was heard to say, "Why would we need her?" Nevertheless, what was a great miracle followed the next day and the weeks after.

Proceeding cautiously that first week, I interviewed a few of the students, made some friends, and read the two-inch-plus thick folders of accumulated background information on each child. Those folders contained every evaluation ever conducted, along with extensive correspondence with parents in America. For the first time I realized the differences between the pain of parents of emotionally disturbed children from that of parents of the mentally retarded. The fact that a child with emotional problems mixes in the community, but often with unpredictable behavior, can be shattering to families. The dangers which deviant behavior can create for both the child and the community are horrible. I could hear the despair of these parents crying out in their letters, describing how much they had suffered. I could sense the relief they felt with their children situated in a half-way house with an intense therapy program.

Questions always arose as to why American parents would send troubled children to a foreign land. The answer was simple: The drug culture and rampant crime had not reached the streets of Jerusalem as they had in cities in America. Parents knew that their vulnerable children could walk the streets safely, day and night. (Unfortunately, today the drug culture has polluted Israel as well, although still on a limited level.)

Slowly, I eased a couple of students into some interesting but non-threatening personality evaluations. They seemed to be fascinated quickly by all of my materials, including the Rorschach cards. Or, I wondered, could it have been my intense interest in them that they liked? In any case, they appeared to know instinctively that they were sharing and leaving a part of themselves with me. They seemed to appreciate my affectionate caring, and were eager to return for more.

By the end of the second week, I was pleasantly surprised when a student knocked on my door and inquired anxiously, "I know I'm supposed to have an appointment with you. When will I have my turn?" Then, some days later, the secretary said to me in amazement, "You know, those kids like you!" I could tell from what the students were saying that many evenings they discussed with each other the time spent with me, and the meaning it had for them. I felt vindicated when, near the end of my stay there, the director reminded me that there were two remaining girls I had yet to see.

There were eighteen students in the school at the time, and I administered intellectual and personality evaluations to each. In addition, I regularly counseled one patient who proved to be different from the others. A former student from New York University, he was a victim of a serious auto accident which left him neurologically impaired. Still a tall handsome youth, his gait, motor skills and speech gave the appearance of a greater intellectual impairment than that which he had really suffered.

Another young man who stood out was a former Johns Hopkins student whose disorientation and neurological impairment were drug related. Although he still gave the appearance of superior intellect, his common sense abilities were severely impaired.

The other youngsters, each diagnosed with another form of psychosis, had problems which I found quite absorbing and gripping. While I was there, one student drowned a cat in a bath tub. One boy attempted to rape another. Still another ran away.

No amount of reading could ever have been so informative as my first-hand observation of the withdrawn, aggressive, and deviant behaviors displayed by these poor youngsters. As a learning experience for me, the school was a marvelous laboratory. In the end, in addition to completing written psychological reports, the director also requested I confer with each student on the results of my evaluation. This proved to be both difficult and rewarding. Deciding what to include in my discussions with these fragile personalities was a constant challenge.

One of the greatest leaps in my learning was my new appreciation of the value of children's drawings. During my course work as a student, I was not convinced that any importance should be placed on drawings. However, as I worked with these youngsters, examining and evaluating their drawings, it all seemed to fall into proper perspective. To my amazement, the bizarre drawings of my emotionally ill clients matched and verified the findings of Freud's teachings about symbolism. Realizing first hand the intrinsic value of symbolism as described by Freud, I developed new awe for his genius.

In the days before we left for the States, I noticed sly smiles on the faces of my young friends. They kept their secret well, and on my last day at the Summit, I was greeted with a huge "Surprise!" They had all contributed to a going away gift, and special refreshments were enjoyed by all! At that point it was difficult to measure which I treasured more from my journey to Jerusalem, the knowledge I had gained, or the friendship of these students.

As an extra bonus, we enjoyed weekly Sabbath reunions with our son and daughter. Each brought friends from their respective schools, so numerous in fact, that we kept a schedule posted on the wall. Their weekly Zemiroth (Sabbath songs) lifted our already delightful and lively Sabbath table to a new height!

After our return, I found another internship placement for the spring semester with the Baltimore County Public Schools, and this added to my preparation in school psychology. However, there was another source of learning which proved invaluable in my training. While I was finishing my course work in 1975, and also while in the Baltimore County internship in 1976, I became eligible for part-time, seasonal work doing pre-school evaluations with programs called "Head Start."

I began with a contracting firm operated by a local psychologist. The stipend was ten dollars each for administering an abridged version of an IQ test offered to pre-schoolers in the Baltimore City schools. There were no reports required, and I was renumerated for as many tests as I could administer. The income from this work was the very first I was to earn in my new profession.

We used the Stanford Binet Form LM, an IQ test which, unfortunately, has never been revised and is now out of use. It had many, many parts to it, and when it was first introduced to us in a testing course, the instructor admitted that even though it was an excellent measure, she did not like using it. At first glance it did appear to be a mind boggling mess of so many different sub-tests and little pieces, and it seemed to take forever to administer. However, if you had to work on an "assembly line" with it, as I did, you could gain speed and come to appreciate this test as truly a treasure for pre-schoolers.

While the contracting firm handled the Baltimore City Head Start classes outside of Baltimore, the Maryland State Department of Education was hiring people to evaluate all of the Head Start pre-schoolers. This part time position paid the princely sum of one hundred dollars per day. However, it was necessary to travel to the far ends of the state, administering a one hour battery of tests to five students each day, administering the entire Binet, a Peabody Picture Vocabulary test, and an evaluation of self-concept.

This evaluation project was headed by a young man, Gene Adcock, whom I had been warned was a strict and exacting taskmaster. On my very first day on the job in one of the distant county schools, he came in to observe me as I tested a little four-year-old boy. We had a conference immediately following the observation, and I had passed with flying colors. Having gained speed working the prior week for the contracting firm had benefitted me. Mr. Adcock commented on my good planning in laying out all the small pieces, and seemed amazed with my accuracy and speed. He even commented about how quickly I produced a tissue for the running nose of my little candidate.

We traveled throughout the state, sometimes signed up for two-or three-day stints, and the State paid for all expenses, putting us up two in a hotel room. Each partner sharing a room had the additional task of checking the other's protocols for accuracy. When I learned that another of the student psychologists preferred to drive the long distance home to Baltimore so that she could spend each night with her family, I joined her eagerly. We had to leave home sometimes as early as six in the morning for the long drive. My driver was Gail Levy, who has remained my friend over the years. Since she had more experience than I, she became my mentor for learning about our responsibilities. I was impressed with her quick, sensible answers to all of my questions, and learned a great deal from her as we drove back and forth.

The schools around the state were very interesting, each with its own personality. I learned quickly that few elementary schools had a special space to evaluate a child, and this often proved a problem. On one occasion, the only place available was in a windowless broomcloset, about six by eight feet. Having no options, I squeezed my small charge between the buckets, mops, and brooms, and sat him at a table there. His immediate response – "Don't put out the light!" – struck me with the comedy of our plight.

With two internships and a part-time work experience under my belt, I was now prepared for my placement in the Baltimore City public schools, in September of 1976.

CHAPTER SEVEN

Hired Under the Wire

As long as a man breathes he should not lose hope.
Jerusalem Talmud Tractate Berakoth 9:1

When I received my Master's degree in January 1976, having completed a year of internship, I sought a tenured position for the September 1976 school year. Positions were scarce that year, and as I applied to different school systems, none were to be found. I turned forty-eight that summer and despaired that I would ever find a school position. When I began applying at the hospitals, I was called back for interviews on three occasions for an opening at Johns Hopkins.

It seemed likely that I would be accepted, but after each interview I went home hoping that they would not hire me. The hospital was a distance from my house, parking was complicated, and the building seemed a labyrinth of corridors. It was nearly August, and I was beginning to lose hope of getting a position in a school.

By a stroke of "luck", an acquaintance told me that there was an opening in Region 2 of the Baltimore City Public Schools, where I had an application on file. I called Mr. Simon Eccard, the head of regional psychological and social work services, and learned he was on vacation. I kept calling and finally reached him on the day he returned. School was opening in less than a couple of weeks, and he was desperate to fill the vacancy. Thus he was delighted that I called, and asked me to come for an interview that very morning.

Mr. Eccard, who became known to me as Simon, proved to be a warm, friendly man, putting me totally at ease. When I arrived he told me that the citywide director of psychological services was on vacation, and that our interview might prove to be "just a stab in the dark." Yet, he was very pleased with all of my papers, and after making a few phone calls to the Central Office, he gave me the job. Miraculously, just under the wire, I had my position in the schools!

During the interview, Mr. Eccard had asked me, "You're in your late thirties?" Taking the female privilege with age, I dishonestly shook my head in the affirmative. Of course, my formal application listed my exact age, which he could have easily verified, but to my knowledge, he never did. I saw him as such a gentle, warm person, and he hugged me as I left. When I arrived home I told my husband that he was the "nicest man I had ever met." Yes, it is true that Orthodox women do not generally accept hugs from unrelated males, yet it was not the last time that I passively accepted a hug in the work place.

It was only later that I learned that the director of psychological services was not happy that Simon had hired me while she was away. However, I do believe that the time came when she realized that I had some worthwhile attributes. In those days there was an entire week of orientation for new staff members. When Simon introduced me to his staff – a friendly group of about twenty-five school psychologists, social workers, and home visitors – he did everything possible to make me feel comfortable. He boasted about my interesting Israel internship, and that my husband was a history professor at Towson. Most of the orientation days were a whirlwind of information about the intricate departments of the school system, with speakers from the central and regional offices.

The speaker who made the greatest impact on me was one who told us of the many children who were suspended from school to school each year. He stressed the role of school psychologists, and that a competent person could save a child who entered our schools from suspension. He pleaded: "It is your responsibility to make such a child feel welcome, to help scourge the child's concept that he or she is unwanted in the schools." I was to remember those words meticulously, and to act upon them in just a matter of weeks.

On one of the orientation days, I left all of my personal belongings, purse, brief case, mountain of handouts, etc., on a seat in the auditorium during a break. When I returned all had mysteriously disappeared. In panic, I searched indoors, out of doors, everywhere I could, seeking help. Finally, a smiling custodian saw me and asked, "Did you lose something?" It seems he saw my materials in the empty room and gathered them into his office, merely to teach me that it was never a good idea to leave anything of value unattended. It was a worthwhile lesson.

Simon, with all of his kindness, placed me in a small school off North Avenue, practically full-time, so that I could get my bearings in my new position. It was to be the beginning of a roller-coaster adventure of ups and downs, agonies and ecstasies, which would last for nearly twenty-five years.

CHAPTER EIGHT

The Boy Who Wanted to Sweep the Hall

The very world rests on the breath of children in the school house.

Talmud Tractate Shabbath 119b

When I entered Mrs. Bright's school on that first day, I was apprehensive of the unknown. However, I was thrilled that my dream was now a reality. I had visions of saving children and helping parents. Even though I was a mature woman with children in college, I had the optimism, vigor, and enthusiasm of a youngster.

As in so many elementary schools, there was no real office available where I could work. So Mrs. Bright settled me at a table in the teacher's lounge, telling me that it would be vacant most of the day. Her manner was cool and abrupt, however, and she seemed to have little interest in speaking to me at all.

The truth of the matter is that she was not happy to have a school psychologist in her school for what appeared to be full time. I suspect now, that in her thinking, this little Jewish lady could be of no help in her school where all the children were of another race. At one point during that first week, she even said, "I'm not going to let you waste my time!" Intimidating as she was, I persisted, as I knew that all referrals needed to come from her.

What I did not realize at first was that Mrs. Bright's school was one of the most efficiently run, orderly, and cleanest that I would ever see. Also, I did not know then that she was a superb administrator, supervisor of teachers, and caregiver for the needs of her students. She had strict standards for herself and expected the same from everyone around her, from her assistant principal to the custodian. She knew what was going on in every classroom, no building repair was completed without her personal direction, and when needed, she made home visits to parents on Saturday mornings. Yet when the tall husky gym teacher told me that she had crushed him with sharp words one day for some fault, I understood that I was not the only one intimidated by her manner.

Mrs. Bright's first referral to me was Melvin (fictional name), who was newly enrolled in a special education class, following suspension from another school. The suspension report noted refusal to remain in his classroom, unexcused absences, and defiance of school rules. In Mrs. Bright's words, he was "vulgar and profane" and the "worst child" she had ever seen. She said that his loud, foul language was such that every student and teacher in the school already knew of him. Her instructions to me were that I must do everything I could to get him out of her school. I did not tell her about the message which the presenter at orientation had etched into my brain:"Yes, it is the responsibility of the school psychologist to make a suspended child feel welcome in his new school. Otherwise he will feel that the world doesn't want him."

Remembering how helpful the confidential folders were with my emotionally handicapped students in Israel, I began by examining Melvin's records. I learned that this eleven-year-old was the eighth child in a family of twelve, many of whom were known to the special training schools for children placed there by the courts for breaking the law. It was reported that as early as age eight he attempted to break into a car with a screwdriver, and that by age ten he had been placed by the court in the Maryland Youth Residential Center for a similar offense. A recent psychological report described him as extremely hyperactive, with a speech defect. His IQ fell within the 70's, meaning that although he was not classified as mentally retarded, his functioning did not reach the low average range. Earlier, a neurologist had prescribed medication for treatment of hyperactivity, but there was no indication it had ever been used.

My next step was to observe Melvin in the classroom. I spent forty-five minutes watching him use all his energy and wits to annoy his teacher and classmates in every way possible. He slapped, pushed and pinched other students, threw books and shrieked loudly and obscenely. When he paused, it was only to rattle his desk and chair vigorously and destructively. I could only agree, that this was a "worst child." I noted, too, that his teacher responded to each of his inappropriate behaviors, and those of his classmates, with screaming, shouting, and scolding.

In my first interview with Melvin, I observed that he was an attractive child of average height and build, despite what appeared to be a slight bulging of the left eye. He told me that his ambition when he grew up was to "clean schools." When I questioned this further, he indicated that sweeping the halls was something he loved to do, and could do best.

Among my routine queries was one about his worst memory, and he responded "to go some place without my mother." I thought immediately of his placement at the Training Center, where he had been separated from his family. At a later interview when I asked why he was absent so much, his spontaneous answer was "I don't read so good!" His words indicated a desperate cry for a change in direction.

While I researched and planned for Melvin, Mrs. Bright still remained pessimistic and critical of my efforts. In fact, I had even more reason to be upset when one day, as we approached the holiday season, she bolted: "Since you like Melvin so much, maybe I should give him to you for Chanuka!" Since no previous reference had been made about my being Jewish, her unexpected rebuke stunned me sharply!

One day I said to Melvin, "When you are with me, you sit so quietly and nicely. How come when I saw you in the classroom you were making so much noise?" I was astounded at his cheerful response, "I like to make the teacher mad. It's fun to have her chase me around the room." He was the only child with whom I ever worked who was clever enough to realize exactly what he was doing, yet naive enough to tell me.

The treasure trove of information which I learned from Melvin about himself set my head swirling with ideas. When I interviewed his teacher, a mildly-plump but pretty and talkative young woman who was new at the school and at teaching, she was beside herself with the problems which faced her. I told her of some of my ideas and she appeared receptive. We began by using a simple behavior plan of check marks for short periods of acceptable behavior. I also gave her some ideas for lowering the noise level of the entire class. I even brought in a bag of candy for her to use as special rewards in order to demonstrate to her how effective praise and reward can be.

After she began implementing my suggestions, her classroom really did quiet down! There was even a small amount of improvement in Melvin's behavior. I then broached the radical new idea: Let him earn time to help the custodian sweep the halls, as rewards for periods of quiet behavior! Although I explained to both the principal and teacher that sweeping the floors was an activity which Melvin would love, Mrs. Bright resisted strongly. It was only after I quoted to her Melvin's words – "It's fun to make the teacher mad" – that she relented.

The custodian, a lovely caring lady, agreed to have Melvin help her. Everyone began to notice that changes were taking place with Melvin. What's more, it took some time, but I also began to notice some changes in Mrs. Bright's attitude toward me.

There was much more work to be done. When I told Mrs. Bright that Melvin was aware that he read poorly, she found a volunteer tutor to work with him privately a couple of days a week. Yet, despite all the strategies, hyperactivity was still an ever-present factor. Thus, the final step was to arrange a new appointment with the neurologist to explore medical intervention. In the end, the principal herself administered this prescribed medication.

With this final piece in place, Melvin miraculously could be now described as a well-behaved, charming, and affectionate child.

By the end of December, his progress could be summed up in a few sentences. He was now a productive member of his class, and his teacher began sharing samples of his good papers. Her screaming at the students was eliminated, and she became a highly effective teacher. I heard third hand that Melvin's mother described this period as the "best in his life." Melvin's left eye no longer bulged, although we had no evidence connecting this physical change to his improved behavior.

It was my greatest pleasure when Mrs. Bright began smiling affectionately when she spoke of Melvin and called him a "sweet child." One day his teacher said to me, "You know you don't have to do anything else in your entire life – you saved Melvin!"

But there was another way in which Mrs. Bright said "Thank you" to me. As we chatted one day about my working with families and students, she used the words "people helping people." I knew it was a new way of thinking for her, and that she now viewed me in the way that I wished to be seen.

There was one other child at Mrs. Bright's school who proved to be an unforgettable learning experience for me, helping me with my future work with parents. He was a first grader newly referred for learning problems, and I administered a psychological evaluation. Afterwards, I felt it would be helpful to him if I could discuss his strengths, weaknesses and fears with his parent. Mrs. Bright informed me that Darrin and his five siblings were in the custody of his grandmother ever since the death of their mother. Knowing her students and parents well, she described this lady – who had no phone – as totally uncooperative. She was certain that there was no way I would ever get her to school for a conference.

She was known to rebuff any efforts of social workers and teachers who contacted her.

Nevertheless, I sent a note home to the grandmother, telling her that I wished to discuss some "nice things about her grandson Darrin," giving a date for an appointment. When the time arrived I did not expect her to attend, and was in another part of the school building. To my surprise, there was a message on the intercom telling me that she had arrived.

As we spoke, I learned from her that her greatest fear was that the authorities would take her six little grandchildren away from her. Now this was my first actual parent conference as a school psychologist, but I believe that all of the "hard knocks" I had received myself from the merciless behavior of professionals evaluating my own handicapped child had taught me instinctively just how to proceed. In any event, I was to learn later that following my conference with Darrin's grandmother, she became a regular visitor to the school, even joining a parent volunteer group.

Soon after, Mrs. Bright invited me to give a brief presentation to the parent volunteer group for whom she had been providing periodic parent training sessions. The attendance worker was also invited to speak, and I was called on first. As a demonstration of the importance of the role of parents, I proudly told the story of how my mother saved me from learning disabilities and failure when I was in first grade. I stressed that even though my mother had no schooling beyond sixth grade, by sharing important information about me with the teacher, she was able to serve as a helpmate to the teacher and to influence my success in school.

Although the audience seemed to enjoy my talk, the inspiring tale told by the attendance worker about the role that her father played during her formative school years far overshadowed my story. It seems that every evening her father, who worked for the railroad, would ask each child in the family to leave completed homework folders piled in a special place for him to check. In addition, he would ask each child to practice reading aloud from a book of directions concerning his work at the railroad. What she did not learn until after her father passed away was this: He had carefully concealed the fact that he had never learned to read himself! The pages which he asked his children to "practice" were his instructions for the following day. Upon hearing that unforgettable ending to her story, I was choking back tears.

During that first year, all the city-wide school psychologists were "redeployed" for a period of two weeks. Our mission was to administer intelligence tests to pre-school children at schools around the city. Considering that I was just getting my bearings that first year, this seemed like an unfair interference. However, the Binet test was used, which few of my colleagues had used widely or mastered. Since I had extensive practice using this at my part-time employment while I was a student, I could breeze through quickly. But reward for my speed was dubious, since I was then called on to complete extra evaluations. Then alas, with that task completed, I was back at Mrs. Bright's school!

Late in December of 1976, we began to hear rumors of budget cuts, which would cause the dismissal of some social workers and school psychologists. Little importance was given to this rumor, so we were shocked when twenty-nine of the most recently engaged service providers – including me – lost their positions at the end of January.

Mrs. Bright would not take this lightly. I listened with disbelief when she told me the Central Office was ready to send her two additional teachers as compensation for losing me, and that she didn't want these teachers – she wanted me! She proceeded to send letters to the School Superintendent, and to other "dignitaries," describing my achievements at her school. She even convened a special parent-teacher meeting asking them to sign a petition for my reinstatement, describing me in quite flattering terms.

But it was all to no avail. On the last day, Mrs. Bright invited all of the teachers to their lounge where I worked, for a sad farewell tribute to me. It was only five months that I worked at her school. During that engrossing time of personal growth, in contrast to my beginnings as a secretary, I ate my bag lunch each day while working at my desk. I would become so immersed in what I was doing that I had no need to stop. My priority – dedication to my students – outdistanced any other pleasures, and my pattern had been set: "No Time For Lunch!"

CHAPTER NINE

And the Teacher Moaned, "I'd Rather Be Scrubbing Floors!"

The bad teacher's words fall on his pupils like harsh rain; the good teacher's, as gently as dew.
Talmud Tractate Ta'anith 7a

After my short career at Mrs. Bright's elementary school, I was unemployed for seven weeks. During that time a series of sensational articles appeared in the Baltimore Sun describing the low achievement and problem behaviors of students at Baltimore City's middle schools. I read them with much interest, and was intrigued by one of the interviews which took place at a southeast middle school. In it, a teacher there, Miss Ganzales (who allowed her name to be used) shrieked to a reporter, "I would rather be scrubbing floors than teaching these miserable, unruly children." Her words remained with me as though I knew that one day our paths would cross…

I finally managed to find another position at a large residential facility for the mentally retarded. However, just one day before I was to report to work, Lois Thomas, head of psychological services at the Baltimore City Schools, phoned with the good news that a new Title One federal project had been funded, chiefly for the benefit of lower-performing middle school children. Five school psychologists were scheduled to be appointed, and those whose positions were eliminated in January were given first choice. I was thrilled at the opportunity to return, and accepted without a moment's hesitation.

This project was titled "Office of Basic Skills," and had an interesting core of workers. Mrs. Marie Francis, wife of a prominent physician, was the project head, and under her were three specialists who served as facilitators in math, reading, and English. Five school psychologists, one social worker, and a score of tutors and aides completed the group. Classes which qualified were selected on the basis of low test scores and impoverished economic levels, and we were permitted to work only with those children who were designated by Title One.

This position began immediately, and within days I was assigned to my new secondary schools, all five of them. It was irrelevant that I had so recently been applauded by my former principal as a highly worthwhile human being and as an accomplished school psychologist. I learned very quickly that I had to prove myself all over, again and again, to the principal and staff of each new school.

One of the schools to which I was assigned was a middle school, and strangely enough, the same one I had read about in the Baltimore Sun. The school was seven stories high, with many difficult-to-monitor stairs and hallways. Because of overcrowding, teachers taught on shift, five classes back to back.

As "luck" would have it, I was assigned to evaluate a child in one of the classes of Miss Ganzales, the very teacher whose words I had not forgotten, alleging that she preferred to scrub floors. It was part of my routine to observe a child in class before a formal evaluation, and Miss Ganzales was totally cooperative. As I sat in her classroom observing my new client, I could not help but see all the problems she was having with all of her students. They arrived late, were out of their seats, and called out. They were a noisy, unruly, and disrespectful bunch. There was never a quiet moment during the forty minutes I was there, and she screamed, criticized, and scolded them non-stop.

That same day, I had a very brief conference with Miss Ganzales, a petite young woman in her twenties. In just a few rushed moments, while standing with her in the hall outside her classroom, I learned a great deal about her and her classes. She herself had been a student at the school, in days when it had been less crowded, and it was there that she became inspired to become an English teacher. However, she was assigned to teach English to only three of her classes, while the other two were designated for remedial reading. The children in the reading classes all had severe reading problems, and as this occurred before federal regulations became effective, special education teachers for these students had been eliminated because of budgetary cuts.

When I heard all of this, my head began spinning with ideas for quieting her classrooms. Teaching five classes back-to-back, of course she had no time to schedule an appointment with me. When I approached her again and again after that to discuss strategies, she would rebuff me briskly telling me that she was too harassed and busy to sit down with me. But, since I could not get her out of my mind, I continued to badger her.

Finally, I bumped into her in the guidance counselor's suite, a large set of offices which I frequented often because the student records were housed there. I sort of backed her into a corner of the office, and told her quickly of my plan to place the children of each class into three groups, giving five points for coming on time, three for raising their hands, and then deducting one point each for calling out and for out-of-seat behavior. I spoke as fast as I could, telling her that at the end of the week the students in the group with the most points could receive extra grade points, individually.

She needed to get back to meet her next group, so there was no time for me to elaborate. Neverless, somehow her face lit up, and she said, "Maybe I will try some new things." Well, based on what happened after that, it was more than her face that lit up, it was as though she experienced some kind of transfusion!

Within a short time she told me, "The students are rushing to my class just to be on time, and after dismissal, they check up to see which group is ahead. They love it!" She told me how thrilled she was to be able to devote time to real teaching. As it happened, initially she had success only with her three English classes. With the lower-performing students, where they focused on remedial reading, group and peer pressure did not seem to work. Thus we revised the plan for them, setting it up for individuals, using the same point system. The student earning the most points each day was named "Student of the Day," and the student with the most points for the week was named "Student of the Week."

In Miss Ganzales' words, this plan "worked fantastically." The head of the guidance department, with whom I had become friendly, knew just a little of my encounter with Miss Ganzales in her office, and commented one day, "Miss Ganzales' classes have taken a complete turn around! How did you do that?" But, the truth of the matter is, I spent so little time teaching her this plan, it was Miss Ganzales – of "scrubbing floors fame" – who accomplished this feat almost by herself.

Another of my five schools was a huge high school located at the other end of town, in the Southwest. Just a few days after arriving there, I happened to be in the main office collecting some information, and chanced to place my folders on the counter which separated the office staff from the students and teachers. The principal came along and asked angrily, "To whom do these materials belong?" When I claimed them as mine, she blurted out, "We do not permit anyone to place anything on this counter!" I should have been warned from that moment of the near-disaster which was awaiting me in that school.

I met each of my Title One teachers in this high school and explained my role, along with the services which I could provide. When I was told of the problems which needed fixing, my head was awhirl with entirely new ideas. What's more, I had never worked in a high school before. There were children needing tutoring, with no tutors available. There were children needing nurturing, due to loss of a parent. There were children who needed help because they were shunned and bullied by their teenage peers.

One of the projects I dreamed up was for peer tutor volunteers to help students who were failing a particular subject. After getting approval from the principal, I discussed this with a couple of teachers. I then met with a group of honor students and many of them volunteered to tutor after school, working one-on-one with those students referred to me by the teachers.

Not too long after implementing the project, I arrived at the high school on my assigned day, and while signing in, was told by the principal that "the meeting" was being held in a conference room two doors from the office. Not being aware of any "meeting", I was really puzzled, and went to the assigned room.

Seated in the room was the Principal, a number of my Title One teachers, the supervisor of psychologists from the Central Office, Dr. Michael Oidick, and one of the specialists from my Title One project. I took a seat next to Dr. Oidick, more puzzled than ever, as the group seemed to be waiting for me. Imagine my shock, when I learned that one of the teachers had complained that I had overstepped my boundaries by initiating the peer volunteer project. It seems that the Principal, in support of the teacher, arranged the meeting and invited my superiors. The only omission was that nobody had informed me, but those friends from the Title I and psychology offices who were there, all assumed that I knew.

When the principal opened the meeting and declared the charge against me – chiefly that I had not obtained her permission for the tutoring project – I was immediately relieved. I had my daily log with me, an hour-to-hour diary of my activities in each school. Referring to my diary, I confidently responded, "But I have a note here that on March 21 I did consult with the Principal, and that she approved. I didn't even know that you were having this meeting today, but I do have this documentation of my activities." The principal, never even asking to see my log, immediately ended the meeting.

The only person to apologize for this fiasco was Dr. Oidick. He was truly shocked that I had not known, and comforted me as well as he could. I also took much comfort when one of the students with whom I had "bonded" thanked me for the tutoring. He was a short, but handsome boy, who did well on the baseball field despite an unfortunate back malformation. He was grieving over the recent loss of his father, explaining: "My father was my best friend. I miss him so much. Getting failing grades in math made everything worse. It was so great that I had a tutor to help me, because now I'm passing math!"

I tried to reason why this teacher, or these teachers, turned against me, complaining to the principal. Much had to do with my being "spread too thin." Having only one day at each school of intimidating size was insufficient, and my days were a constant rush, rush, rush! In addition to "no time for lunch", perhaps I suddenly had no time for kind words for harassed teachers. Over the faculty lunch table, the setting was conceivably ripe for hurt feelings to seethe into anger against me in the full week until I returned.

Although Marie Francis did not acknowledge verbally the embarrassment which this high school had caused me, she did write a gracious note to Dr. Oidick, with a copy to Lois Thomas:

"On May 11, 1977 I had the opportunity to visit Earson High School, where Mrs. Blumberg is currently working. I met the administrative, teaching, and support personnel assigned to that school. I was extremely pleased to learn that Mrs. Blumberg had initiated a peer tutoring program, which is desperately needed in schools like Earson for improving students' basic skills. Even though this project was begun relatively late in the school year, I understand its impact has been beneficial for several students, and it is felt that this type of approach has considerable potential for next year."

When the school year ended, Marie Francis informed us that there was to be a week scheduled for staff development for all teachers and aides working on the Title I project. I was startled to learn that the five psychologists, the lone social worker, and three specialists, were to be the presenters at this week-long workshop.

My assignment was a two-hour presentation to about one hundred teachers, on any topic which I selected. Luckily we had a couple of weeks in between school ending and the date of our workshops, and I spent nearly a full week at home preparing. My two young psychologist friends, who were as new to this as I, begged me to join them for a group presentation. I wisely preferred to work alone, however, feeling I could handle my own unpredictability, but would not be able to handle theirs. The seeming handicap of my past fears of public speaking, still very much with me, drove me to organize in depth a well-researched program about behavior management. I prepared as though my life depended on this. It included overhead projections, original handouts, and jokes, ending with a group participation activity for all of those present. As a bonus, I was confident that I had a useful document for the future.

For my group activity, I asked the teachers to identify classroom behaviors with which they were concerned, and I listed them on a chalk board as they spoke. I then asked each teacher to put in writing one or more of her favorite strategies for any of the behaviors listed on the chalk board. The response was so beautiful, that I was able to set them aside until a later date, and with some editing, put them into an in-house twenty-five page document!

Following my address, a few of the teachers with whom I had become friendly during the workshop week gave high praise to my talk. What none of them realized was that in my mind, it was a marvel that I did this at all. However, the greatest satisfaction was that my vision of saving children and helping parents and teachers had become a reality!

Thus, my first year with the Baltimore City Public Schools came to an end. It was a roller coaster year crammed with ups and downs, and loaded with many lessons which might have made my future experiences in the schools a breeze.

CHAPTER TEN

Charmed By Baltimore's Neighborhoods and People

Why was man created a solitary human being without a companion? So it could never be said that some races are better than others.
Talmud Tractate Sanhedrin 37a

It was easy to see that with the opening of the fall semester of each year, the only certainty was that changes would occur. The change that mattered most to me that year was that our project would no longer service the high schools. It was felt that the younger the student, the greater the impact, an idea which seemed to make much good sense. Whether my own embarrassing experience at the high school during the previous year played any role in that decision, I don't know.

My three assigned middle schools, all located in different parts of town, provided an interesting variety. Coming from the northern states, I always considered myself a newcomer to Maryland, with much to learn about the city of Baltimore. Thus, I was struck in those days with the fascinatingly diverse populations in my three schools. Each was a considerable distance from the other, located in the southeast, southwest, and northwest areas of Baltimore.

Hampstead Hill, the southeast school where I first met the teacher of "scrubbing floors fame" was still mine. This neighborhood was called Highlandtown, and I had been hearing for years about the white stone steps of its row houses, and how housewives there scrubbed these steps each day. Now, while driving to work each day, I was thrilled to see block after block of these neat streets which had long been populated by families of European descent. The front windows of some of the houses had screens with paintings on them, something I had never seen before.

Since this was the late seventies, the school – which was now mixed racially – still had some of the older staff members from the time when the school was a segregated white school. It interested me, that in those days, no matter how unique, complex, or bizarre the family problems of some of my white students at Hampstead Hill were, their children were sent to school with a clean, scrubbed look. At the same time, an African American parent at the school once related to me that the people of Highlandtown, no matter what their race, are different from other people. There may have been some truth to what she said.

My office at Hampstead Hill was located in the health suite. Since nurses were then being phased out of the schools as full time support members, this health suite was the first of many which I was to occupy during my tenure in the schools. A wall of windows blasted sunshine onto my desk, and it was nice to watch how fast my plants grew, even during the short days of winter.

Sharing the suite with me was the head of a project which provided support services for descendants of native American Indians. She herself was a member of an Indian group, had earned a Ph.D. in health science, and as we became friendly, she acquainted me with her project and the needs of her clients. This was the closest I had ever come to learning about the native Indians of the Maryland area, and I loved hearing all that I could from her.

My second school, Harlem Park, was located in southwest Baltimore, and it provided an interesting contrast. Whereas Hampstead Hill occupied an old building seven stories high, Harlem Park was a newer building with fewer floors but as many students, spread out via numerous wings. Because of the size and large sprawling territory it covered, each grade – seventh, eighth, and ninth – existed as a separate entity.

One day Marie Francis, our Title I project head, tried to reach me by calling the main office of the school. When the secretary could not find me, Mrs. Francis tried many different phone extensions and still had no success. As I was usually "findable" at my schools, she became concerned that I had become ill, or even worse, had been "mugged." She even phoned my husband at home. He reassured her, telling her that he had learned from a past anxious experience of his own that it is not unusual to "lose" me in a school. Such was the size of Harlem Park.

At that time, Harlem Park was also a school of mixed races. The whites there, however, were very different from those in the southeast part of the city. Many were more recent migrants to Baltimore, likely from the mountain and rural areas of nearby southern states. Perhaps because we were still in the days immediately following integration, or for some other reasons which I cannot totally understand, the two racial groups at Harlem Park were not always harmonious. It was a mood which even permeated members of the staff. One of the African American guidance counselors once protested to me about a white student whom she was attempting to help, saying "Oh, he's such a nasty child, and doesn't like working with me because I'm Black." Since I knew him too, I was able to make a declaration which I was to repeat again and again, to both my white and black colleagues: "It only seems that way. Actually, he has so many serious learning and behavioral limitations that he hasn't even noticed that you are of a different race!" I had learned this truth in observing parents in the support groups which I attended as a parent of my own profoundly handicapped child.

In those days the counselors in my middle schools, many of them African Americans, were very warm and welcoming to me. Those who were considerably older than I and near the end of their careers, had grown up the hard way, in the Jim Crow days. They confided in me readily, telling me of ordeals which they endured when they were younger, all of which were startling to anyone who grew up in the North.

One counselor told me of an episode which took place while working in a factory during World War II. She said that one day a white co-worker passed around a bag of candy and when it came her turn, the colleague separated a piece in the bag so that my friend's fingers would not touch the other pieces. Another told me about the obstacles faced in those days with shopping, as white clerks turned their backs, ignoring her. I was shocked to learn that she had to travel to Philadelphia in order to buy a new dress, because the department stores in Baltimore would not permit her to enter the fitting rooms.

At Harlem Park I shared an office with a beautiful young African American woman who wore stunning clothing. She was tall and slender, with a lovely figure, and looked more like a fashion model than an attendance worker. A divorcee with one child, she lived in her parents' home in a nice suburb. Being younger, she represented a contrast from my older black guidance counselors who had grown up in more trying times. She was good company and we enjoyed sharing tales about ourselves.

As we became closer, one day she compared her life's circumstances to mine, indicating that she had no husband to support her, a less lucrative college degree, and very little security. The next time we were together I made a special effort to tell her about my son, Michael, and of all that we had been through and still faced. Her expression changed as I spoke, and she responded, "I guess things are not always the way they seem. A person can be much better off than they realize!"

It would be dishonest to say that when I first entered the schools, I didn't have my own thoughts about being a minority white person in a mostly Black system. I even wondered what would happen to me should my car run into problems deep in the inner city. But, I needn't have worried. During the first year alone there were three occasions when African Americans who were total strangers came to my rescue.

One wintry day a neighborly man came out of his house with a shovel to extricate my car from the ice. Others have pushed my car off the ice on a parking lot, and once I was driven to a nearby auto repair shop. I had frequent thoughts that I might not have received such kind treatment from some of the neighbors on my own street.

There was something else which I observed on days when I parked my car on the street a distance from the school. As I walked the one or two blocks, the African American householders would usually greet me with a friendly smile and "Good Morning," only as people do in small towns. The same friendliness evidenced itself when I met Black colleagues at the mall, and it always made me feel good when these acquaintances greeted me with a warm hug.

It would be dishonest, too, to say that I didn't have my own observations of some of the impoverished white families which I met at both my southeast and my southwest schools. Of course, as I only saw children who had problems; I was never in touch with any of the higher-performing regular education students. Thus, my perceptions may be very skewed. However, some of the family problems of the white children with whom I worked appeared to me to be really bizarre.

Back in Highlandtown, the southeast neighborhood with the white stone steps, a mother of a fourteen-year-old white boy who was socially withdrawn and who had failing grades, revealed something startling to me. I knew from my own evaluation of her son that he harbored thoughts of cruel aggression. Thus, I was astounded when she told me that her husband had purchased a large hunting rifle for the boy. "The rifle" she related, "is standing in a corner of one of the bedrooms, waiting to be given to him as a reward when his grades improved."

In 1975 a remarkable new Federal Law, PL 142, was passed in order to insure the rights of handicapped students. In the past, many students with disabilities had been overlooked because of lax testing, never receiving any special services. As it took some years to fully implement the new law, by the late seventies there were still many residual cases of children whose handicaps had not yet been uncovered.

One of these overlooked students was thrust into my life in a most unusual way. A teacher came to me one day, quite excitedly, saying that a seventh grade girl told the class, in a loud voice, that she had been raped the day before. The teacher related that all the students were in shock by the bold way in which the girl disclosed this to the entire class. "You must see her and help her!" the teacher pleaded.

I saw her that day, but using all of my best interview skills, learned little about a rape. Whenever I asked what worried her most, or what kinds of things made her sad, her response was, "I can't read!" Finally, I gave her a quick reading test, and sure enough, this seventh grader was reading with much difficulty at a low first grade level. Within some days I gave her an intelligence test and my suspicions were verified. She had an IQ in the lower sixties, in the range of mild mental retardation.

Upon further investigation, it was discovered there was no rape. It was my conclusion that her poor social skills and her wish to be noticed were such that the "rape" provided a quick means of getting the attention of her peers. We were then able to proceed with placing her in a special class where she might enjoy some success at her level. Unfortunately, it is not unusual in any school system that a quiet, well-behaved child may have serious problems which go unnoticed for many years.

My third school that year was Greenspring Middle, a new building about three miles from my home. I learned early that each of my schools had its own personality, which was similarly apparent in human beings. Such was the case with my northwest school.

My office at Greenspring was lovely and carpeted. I even had my own phone. This was pure luxury. It was my only school which comprised a totally African American population; interestingly, in comparison to my other two schools, everything there, building, staff, teachers, and students gave a feeling of a higher level of prosperity. The teachers and support staff were all friendly and lovely to work with. Yet for me, there was a tension which I could not explain for some time. However, I was immediately aware that, unlike my other schools, there were no windows at all in the building. In fact, when it snowed, the lone window in a stairway was plasticized in such a way that one could not see the snow falling.

At first I gave little thought to being in a windowless building. Then, one day I realized when I came out of the building after school, that as the sunshine and daylight hit my face, I underwent a feeling of physical and psychological revival. It was as though I was touched by a wand which lifted my spirits.

I began to wonder why I did not feel that way when I left Hampstead Hill, the antique, shabby building in southeast Baltimore, far from my home. Then I thought of the cheerful wall of sunlight which came in through the windows there in the health suite where I worked. I realized for the first time the importance of daylight and sunshine. The thought of hundreds of students and their teachers cooped up in windowless environments for five days each week was quite oppressive. It was the beginning of an explanation for the tension which I felt in that otherwise beautiful Greenspring School building.

Each week I wove my way through the interesting neighborhoods of Baltimore, serving the Title One children and teachers at my three schools, and attending Marie Francis' meetings. I kept learning more and more about ways to help my students and their teachers. I would need every skill I could assemble in order to tackle the challenges which lay ahead of me in the middle schools.

CHAPTER ELEVEN

Helping Teachers and Kids Like Each Other

A pupil receives a fifth of the reward that accrues to a teacher.

Midrash Song of Songs Rabbah

One of the many things which I have always enjoyed about my profession was that no matter how much knowledge I gained, there was always so much more to learn. Why people behave as they do had always intrigued me. Thus, exploring personality features, a mainstream challenge of school psychology, became my favorite endeavor. I took pride in my ability to uncover the innermost thoughts of a child's mind. I enjoyed using the marvelous tools we have for measuring personality features, all of which require exquisite refinement of skill and judgment, albeit some subjectivity. Using these techniques I often felt as though I had my own magic mirror, and that as I held it up to a child's mind, I could unfold pictures of that child's thoughts, fears, and self-concept. Those moments of revelation rewarded me with profound satisfaction, because I felt more empowered to help them. Why, even now, as an older member of the Kiryat Arba community, I remain preoccupied with why people behave as they do!

In addition, I devised my own set of interview questions early on, taking them from a number of different sources. Many of my young clients rewarded my efforts by confiding private thoughts, followed with the avowal, "I have never told that to anyone" or "I never before said that out loud!" The eyes of my student might swell from sudden tears of relief, and at these tender moments, I knew that my student and I became as one. I knew that these moments mirrored my evolution into a religious being.

Thus, as I explored my three middle schools, it was easy for me to mediate conflicts between individual students and teachers. When teachers referred their unruly students to me, I noted the disdain in their voices for some of the children. Then, when interviewing the child, it became obvious that the feeling was mutual. I was determined to improve these relationships.

One of the teachers once told me that a student disliked her so much that he sat sideways so he wouldn't have to look at her. And sure enough, as he sat with me, there he was sitting almost with his back to me. The teacher seemed surprised when I told her of this. I then explained to her that his self-concept was so lacking that any kind of eye contact was difficult for him. And so, there it was again: "Things aren't always what they seem!"

I liked to ask students what kinds of things I could tell their teachers about them that would be helpful. Responses like "I don't like to be called on when I don't know the answer," "She never gives me a chance to be a helper," or "She always picks on me," were easy to relate back to the teacher.

Once one of the teachers demanded that a boy in her class apologize to her for some offensively rude language which he used addressing her. It took much manipulation and rehearsal with this stubborn child, but it was a great satisfaction to her when he apologized.

Most of my young clients were males, and for some reason I enjoyed them more than the girls, at least at the Middle Schools. When some of these young teen age males became attached to me, I would ask myself, "Why in the world do they want to spend time with me?" And as these non-compliant adolescents who created fear in others relaxed in the haven of my office, I saw that race proved absolutely no hindrance in any success which I enjoyed.

My young clients were sometimes able to reveal my own frailties. An eighth grade girl with whom I had worked only briefly, once came into my office in great anger flinging her school books on my desk, then screamed, "When I am with you, you act as though you really like me, and that I am your best friend. Well, I saw you in the hall during class change, and you wouldn't even look at me and say 'Hello'! You don't really care about me at all!" I knew immediately what had happened. The halls are crowded and noisy during class change, and I simply didn't see her. Also, I am too often so engrossed in thought that it is not unusual that I miss greeting people whom I know. I promised myself I would try to change my behavior and look at the faces of the children as I walked the halls, lest I offend another young friend.

It was not unusual that a staff member, when discussing a student would say, "Oh, he won't work with you, he's too mean!" I always felt what they were really saying was, "You are too gentle for this rough boy; you will not know how to handle him." It was my great satisfaction that I always proved them wrong.

The most frequent complaint which I heard from the teachers of these low-performing students in the Title I project was about large scale behavioral disruptions involving entire groups. Thus, improving the behavior of whole classes became a target of concentration.

Although I had success the previous year at Hampstead Hill with Miss Gonzales my "scrubbing floors" teacher, I discovered that I still had much to learn. Whereas Miss Gonzales needed little direction once I gave her a rough outline of a plan, other teachers seemed to need far more guidance. Furthermore, I learned that this process only worked with young teachers, and that those set in their ways had more difficulty with the new ideas. I found myself sounding off like a salesperson with a product to sell, and that is exactly what I was! I had to "sell" them on the idea that I could help them entice their students to raise their hands, stay in their seats, and listen to instructions. I was thoroughly convinced of the superiority of my product, "behavior management," and I pushed it with fiery enthusiasm.

But there was another challenge facing me. I realized that most of the materials that I used were for the elementary schools. Thus, I really had to search, revise, and invent, as I collected my storehouse of ideas for my Middle School children.

At one time I had classroom projects going in each of my three schools. Each had to be tailor-made for varying teacher needs and circumstances. At Harlem Park one cluster of teachers – English, Science, Social Studies, and Math – taught the same five classes, the lowest performing seventh graders of the school. The behaviors selected by the teachers to improve were: cutting class, tardiness, fighting, and class work completion. Each class could earn up to ten points for each target behavior successfully modified during each period by all of the students. Since points could not be earned unless all the students showed the proper behavior, peer pressure was an important factor. The class earning the most points could earn a group reward at the end of the week, such as viewing a film, a free-reading library period, or time for board games.

The teachers reported that the project was successful immediately with three of the highest classes. However, with the two lower classes, there was little success. We then placed each of these students on an individual point card. Each could earn one point for any target behavior, each period. At the completion of fifty points, the card was redeemable for a reward. Within three weeks of the revision, all of the teachers were pleased. These lowest performing students began asking for work. Those who never brought notebooks began to bring them. Grades improved. The enthusiasm of the students was overwhelming and spread to the teachers. In the words of one, "It's like something magic has happened!"

At Greenspring Middle School, only one of the Title I staff, the math teacher, was in a state of despair over her non-compliant students. She felt the need for help, but only with three of her five classes. In this case, rather than total classes competing with each other, we divided each class into three groups. Each group could earn up to ten points for success in each behavior. Points were recorded on the blackboard, and rewards were dispensed to one group in each class on Friday. The group with the most points could play math games on Friday.

After four weeks the students were told that following the next four-week period, the class with the highest total points would be permitted to see a film. This gave the groups which never won an opportunity for a reward, and was used in conjunction with the weekly group reward. Other revisions were use of a kitchen timer set to go off unexpectedly twice each period. If all the members of a group were in their seats and at work when the timer sounded, bonus points were awarded to that group. Also, there was a special incentive for handing in homework. All the names were put into a box (one box for each group), two names were chosen from each box, and if both of the two had his homework, the group earned a bonus. This was done as often as the teacher desired.

Sure enough, the mood of the teacher at Greenspring was soon transformed from one of despair to pleasure, as her students responded. Good reports from my teachers spurred me on. When any revision was required, I would not be content until I found some solution. I might wake up in the middle of the night thinking about what to do next, and sometimes my best ideas came to me then.

My husband and children became accustomed to hearing detailed stories of my current student and teacher crisis. Fortunately they found them intriguing, remembering until today some that I may have forgotten. Of course, as every fully-employed Jewish Sabbath-observing mother knows, cooking and preparing for the Sabbath are completed during weekday evenings. In fact during the short days of winter, my Sabbath table was always set by Thursday evening.

I became euphoric when so many of my students began improving in behavior and performance, and I carried my elation back to our meetings at the Title I project office. My successes made me feel seven feet tall! Of all the psychologists, my friend Beverly Cooper-Brown was most interested, and she and I sat for long periods consulting and devising.

What I did not realize was that the educational facilitators, who served as assistants to our director Marie Francis, had other thoughts about what I was doing. One day as I sat at a table working with the three facilitators, women of ability and confidence, one of them began to berate behavior management. She was quite negative, and brought to the surface all of the challenges which naysayers hold. Her chief criticism was, "Why should we 'bribe' students to do what they should be doing anyway?" Each in turn added comments as: "Behavior modification is not an acceptable teaching method!" and "The improvements seen are not lasting gains!" In my over-active perception, they seemed bent on crushing me down to size.

Never quick to respond to verbal attack, I said very little. However, inside I seethed with hurt and anger. I spoke to no one about this attack, but brooded silently for some days. Finally I had a solution. I would put in writing a small handout about behavior management, as a sort of teaching tool for all the members of the Title I project.

I sat down to compose this at home, spending all my free time on it. It grew and grew into a "How To" manual of eighteen pages, and even sported a table of contents. It began with rules for teachers, rules for therapists, samples of point cards, rewards, and other useful forms. Next, I described five different projects with which I had had success. It closed with three pages explaining the rationale and justification of using these techniques. One of these pages was titled "Is Reinforcement Bribery?" which of course was directed to my critic who had crushed me so painfully at the Title I office.

Since this all took place in the days before computers, I typed it at home on my beautiful IBM electric typewriter. The two secretaries at the Title I office who were always so kind to me, xeroxed and collated my manuscript. I never had even the faintest dream I would one day become a published author, nor did it ever occur to me that I had produced a document which could be published. I placed a copy in the mailbox of each of my Title I colleagues. I was proud of my work, and I was certain that the response from the facilitators would be a pleasant one.

To my chagrin, I did not know then that colleagues do not appreciate handouts of this sort. It is an activity which I would not recommend, as it appears to others as an intimidating, competitive, and a "show off" kind of exercise. Thus, I waited what seemed like many days, and the only acknowledgment of any kind came from one of my fellow psychologists, who told me that I had misspelled a word. I began to despair that it wasn't very good at all.

But, at last, the wind changed direction! A couple of weeks later, I was working alone in a room with Judy Torner and Gail Levy, my fellow psychologists, whom I saw infrequently. They began heaping lavish praise upon my booklet. Their enthusiasm was all that I needed. I realized that mature colleagues do not let petty jealousies cloud the way, and at that moment, I felt they were my only friends on the project. If my encounter with them had not taken place, I might never have had the courage to write another piece.

In total the year proved to be a foundation stone for the many more things which I still needed to learn about school psychology, the Baltimore schools, and about dealing with colleagues.

CHAPTER TWELVE

I Learn Some Magic

Much have I learned from my teachers, more from my colleagues, but most from my students.
Talmud Tractate Ta'anith 7b

As September rolled in, the changes in our Title I project, plus enrollment in a class which provided refinement for my behavior management skills, proved to be of great significance for me. I was able to play a new, important role in the lives of many maladjusted boys who were on perilous routes of destruction for themselves and others. Instead, I succeeded in turning them into model students.

As part of an experiment devised by our project head, Marie Francis, I was to be assigned only one school for the Fall semester, the beautifully adorned, windowless Greenspring. For the Spring semester, I was to work full-time at my familiar Hampstead Hill. The rationale was that working in the same school every day of the week might provide better service. For me it was to be to be an entirely new and exciting experience. The value of providing vital support and continuity by seeing the most disruptive children daily, proved to be enormous.

Coupled with this, by "chance" good timing, I was presented an opportunity to refine my behavior management skills. While at a meeting of the approximately fifty Baltimore city-wide school psychologists, there was an announcement about a "family-oriented hands-on behavior management project." An unusual program, it was to be given by Dr. Sam Berkowitz, a psychologist at a local facility, the Regional Institute for Children and Adults (RICA). My friend Beverly Cooper-Brown, whose interests in behavior mirrored mine, joined me, and we enrolled enthusiastically. Thus, my opportunity to see children on a daily basis, coupled with the improved behavior skills I learned, provided me new heights for success and personal enjoyment.

The class met on Wednesday evenings, from five until nine. Despite the late hour after a regular working day, the approach was so stimulating that I devoured every minute of it. The time format was cleverly arranged, so that half of the session was allotted for us to advance our knowledge of theory, and the other, to meet with actual clients.

There were lectures by Dr. Berkowitz and inspiring films of actual case studies, demonstrating the value of behavior management. There were handouts of a number of wonderful new forms which outdid those I had devised myself. Because behavior management is deceptively simple and only works when all rules are followed, Dr. Berkowitz was meticulous with teaching theory to the participating parents also. They spent half of their two-hour session in groups, while the children did other things, where he offered upbeat lectures and films to build enthusiasm for following the rules of behavior management. During the last hour, each family met privately with their counselors.

Each student was assigned a family for counseling, and the family assigned to me consisted of a young, white, blue-collar couple and their twelve-year-old, very rebellious son, Barry. They had been referred to RICA by the guidance counselor at Barry's Baltimore County middle school. Reportedly he resisted following school rules, was disrespectful to teachers, and aggressive toward peers.

Dr. Berkowitz had two student assistants who monitored the process with the family. The assistant assigned to me, upon my meeting with my client family, immediately produced a "Daily Progress Report." I had seen similar forms before, which were called "conduct sheets." Never before had I seen one which could serve as such a complete, implicit, quick diary of a student's day, as this one did.

It was "love at first sight" the moment I saw that piece of paper. It had a space for teachers to enter a grade of "poor, good, or excellent" for behaviors that were selected, such as "on time for class, brought materials, homework completion, conduct and cooperation." There was also a space for teachers to add special remarks and for parents to sign and write comments.

Barry was given enough copies for each day of the coming week, to be completed and returned to us the following week. This information provided us with a base line, or beginning point, and we were then able to set up our program of rewards and penalties. When I began to see the changes in Barry's teachers' comments in the following weeks, I couldn't wait to begin using this method with the students in my own schools.

My newly refined behavior modification skills, coupled with the freedom to see my clients daily rather than weekly, supplied me with undreamed of opportunities to help students. Among the many children whose behavior I was able to reverse that year, the events of two remain most remarkable. They were two fourteen-year-old disruptive boys, both of whom were on a dangerous path of self-destruction.

The first of my two most remarkable clients was Calvin. When Mr. Mazer, the assistant principal at Greenspring referred him to me, he sounded despondent as he described this child who "ran the halls every day during class time," a child for whom he had "no hope." When I first met Calvin, I thought to myself, "What a strange, aloof-appearing little kid!" The most striking things which I discovered from his cumulative records were that as early as kindergarten, he had posed major classroom problems and was already physically aggressive with his pre-school peers.

Even though Calvin was very eager to see me every day, according to the behavior slips during the first week, we were making no dent in his bad behavior. In fact, he was "losing" his behavior forms almost every day. Finally I asked, "Calvin, what kind of reward would you like most?" He thought for a while, and I was stunned and amused when he responded, "A lollipop?" As he said these words, a new revelation came to me, and I melted as I thought, "Calvin is a fourteen-year-old teenage boy, but inside his mind, he is only a baby."

However, following his direction carefully, I promised him a lollipop, to be awarded if just one of the teacher comments showed any improvement at all. After three days, he came to me with his improved form, and told me – all smiles and with much exuberance and pride - "This is the longest I have ever kept up anything in my entire life!" At that moment, I knew I was hooked with the use of the Daily Progress Report, and from then on, I viewed it as a "magic piece of paper."

At that time, I began to convey my thoughts to Mr. Mazer and his teachers about my new perception of him as a "baby" rather than a teenager. Also I began my search into the depth of his anxieties. It seemed the thing he feared most both in school and in his neighborhood was the taunting of his peers. I learned that he suffered great pain from the fact that his father was known on the streets as an out-of-bounds alcoholic. To his credit, however, Calvin had adequate academic ability, and he began to improve in every way. As he no longer roamed the halls, he performed well in class. Somehow a mutual, fond attachment between Calvin and me grew, and I could no longer remember why I found him strange and aloof upon our first meeting.

No Time for Lunch

Although Mr. Mazer began to view me as a worker of magic, Calvin's story does not have a happy ending. Since my schedule had been set to spend only the Fall semester at Greenspring, and then at Hampstead Hill for the Spring semester, the time came for me to move. Although there was a vague, built-in opportunity to continue visiting at Greenspring, it was not equal to being there every day. Thus, when the end of January arrived, I began to prepare Calvin for my departure. I told him that I regretted having to leave, but that it was something over which I had no control. I tried, to no avail, to find a replacement for myself within the school. I tried to find a "Big Brother" from outside the school, as I had done for many other students, only to learn again that their waiting list was far too long. I thought I did my best with explaining this to him, but it was not sufficient.

On one of my less frequent visits to Greenspring to check up on my students there, I was heartbroken to hear that Calvin was absent frequently, and that his behavior had retrogressed. Finally, I caught up with him one day and began exploring what was really going on. Suspecting that my departure had something to do with his decline, I asked him pointedly about what he saw as the problem. While he sat there saying nothing, he pointed his finger, accusingly and directly, at me. I repeated that I had no control about leaving Greenspring, and then I was stunned when he repeated to me the thoughtless and untrue words of a staff member: "Your bad behavior is the reason that Mrs. Blumberg left Greenspring!"

I felt heartsick and devastated with this turn of events. I tried to do what I could to mend the situation, but I have never felt satisfied. That he was more emotionally fragile than I had anticipated, and that I was not able to find an adequate replacement for the attachment which he had for me, were sad facts.

I have never totally resolved the real problems here. When a child attends a clinic outside the school, I have observed that it is not unusual that this outside therapist frequently cannot change any disruptive school behaviors in the same manner as a school psychologist, who is "on the scene" every day. Also, I am aware of the problems of "over dependency" by clients, and that some of them remain with the same therapist for a period of years. Furthermore, as my position was funded by a federal project, there was just no one available to replicate the time and attention I was able to devote to Calvin.

I Learn Some Magic

My school for the Spring term, my own Hampstead Hill, was located a diagonal ten mile drive across town to the southeast of my house in the northwest. Never one to enjoy driving on the expressway during rush-hour traffic, I left home at 7:00 each morning, taking my breakfast with me, to avoid the rush-hour traffic.

I met my second most remarkable student soon after my arrival at Hampstead Hill, when Billy was referred to me. Like others, I was told he was "the worst child" in their "Chapter One" middle school program. As the child of a single parent, Billy had recently been returned to his mother's care after spending most of his years in a total of four different foster homes. He was a blond, blue-eyed child, short for his 13 years, and very slender. Although reports indicated average to high-average intellectual potential, he was a low achiever, and was on medication for hyperactivity. His grade level with spelling, his weakest area, was five years below that expected of someone his age.

His behavior was so disruptive that his teachers were certain he was seriously emotionally disturbed. A review of his earlier evaluations, however, suggested that he suffered from a learning-disability. Because his behavior had prompted nothing but scolding and punishment all of his life, Billy genuinely believed he could never behave appropriately in school.

When I first met Billy in February, he had already failed all subjects for the first semester and had received "Unsatisfactory" in conduct on all of his report cards. Classroom behaviors included constantly talking and interrupting the teachers, daily altercations with peers, and scratching his own arms and face until they bled. It was reported that Billy's mother was so discouraged with his frequent disciplinary removals from school that she spoke of returning him to foster care.

In the beginning of implementing my program using my "magic piece of paper," the DPR, the teachers were not very enthusiastic or cooperative. They were certain I was engaged in a useless battle, and that Billy could not improve in any way. In fact, one of the male teachers became so angry with Billy one day that he left his class unattended, traveling two floors below to my office, to vent his anger against me. When I met with all the teachers, there was open indifference and resistance to my strategies.

However, my confidence with my improved and refined strategies was so high, there was no way that they could deter me. I started Billy off by allowing him to earn material awards, such as school supplies. I then gradually shifted to more innovative prizes, geared to his specific interests.

For instance, when I learned that he loved maps, I collected all of my old AAA maps and doled them out one by one, as his behavior improved. Also, each week I allowed him to select a good behavior certificate of his choice. Later, I learned that he had decorated a wall of his bedroom with these certificates. When behaviors were particularly good, I took him to administrators of his choice to let him "show off" all of the favorable teacher comments. I conferred with teachers, who became more receptive as behaviors improved, reminding them to express words of praise when writing approving comments.

One day I had a backup of students waiting in my office and in my haste, I skipped something important on Billy's DPR. "Excellent +++" had been marked in the column for conduct. When he brought this to my attention, I was struck with its importance to him, and I was elated to have played a part in helping him achieve success.

But the greatest triumph of all followed a meeting which I had with Billy's mother, about half-way through the semester. As we discussed Billy's improved behavior and grades, I emphasized the importance of acknowledging to him her pleasure with these changes. The very next day when Billy came to see me, I could see an unusual expression of calm contentment on his face. I knew immediately that he had something special to tell me, and when he described the moving but simple event which had transpired between him and his mother, I was astounded.

He began by telling me that when he entered his living room after school, his mother was sitting there in semi-darkness. He began very slowly, as though he wished to savor every moment of the event. It seems his mother then beckoned him to come closer. As he did, she reached out her arms and held him close to her, wordlessly, hugging him tightly. I listened in amazement and almost disbelief, as I realized that perhaps this was the first time in his memory that his mother had ever hugged him.

By the end of the semester, Billy's conduct was excellent, he no longer scratched his arms and face, and he passed all subjects. The profound feelings of euphoria which I enjoyed with helping to change Billy's life can be described best as "an experience of reverence."

CHAPTER THIRTEEN

A New Beginning

The world is new to us every morning – that is G-d's gift, and a man should believe he is reborn each day.

Baal Shem Tov

A couple of years later rumors began to fly that the Chapter I project would no longer be funded. As I began to think of my options, I decided that returning to a regional office would be my preference. It was a simple matter to apply for this, and the region of my choice – Region Five in the Northwest – was granted.

When I returned to the region it was my entry into a new world. There were many pluses, and my case load would be expanded, in view of the kinds of children I would see.

Instead of servicing only low-performing middle school children, I would now be working with students from pre-school through high school, identifying and serving those with suspected problems. Each regional office employed social workers and home visitors, as well as school psychologists, providing me with new opportunities to interact with peers. I felt stimulated and excited by it all.

It was the custom on days when we were scheduled for meetings at the Regional office, for colleagues to lunch out. Feeling pressure to accept when invited, at first I joined, albeit apprehensively. For one thing, in those days there were no kosher restaurants in Baltimore. Thus, my choice of lunch – cold garden salads and beverages – seemed to create a stir among my new friends. Those who were Jewish, but who had no understanding of what constituted kosher food, had their own ideas and advice about what I could order. Others just shook their heads in dismay. Thus, my original proclivity towards "No Time for Lunch" chiefly as a robber of children's precious needs, made it easy for me to refuse luncheon invitations.

The regional office served as a home base, and fortunately my new Region Five was located only a couple of miles from my actual home. Supposedly each worker was to have a desk at this home office, but it was a scramble that first week to find one which afforded some kind of privacy.

The head of this pupil service team was Mary Reid, a social worker of much distinction. She was full of charm, kindness, and wisdom, and had a keen intelligence. She was highly devoted to her employees and the students, and most of all, had an inner grace such as I have rarely encountered. An African American woman in her early sixties, she was mildly plump and of medium height. Although I could not have realized her greatness at our first meeting, it was soon after that I discovered the depth of beauty within her. Her words were always carefully expressed and deliberate, and were delivered in a deep but distinctively soft voice, whether speaking to an individual or to a large group.

In the early weeks I was to see her in action at one of my new schools. One of the principals, a most capable lady, had some concerns because many directives of the new school year had changed. I privately questioned why she would be surprised at any of the inevitable changes that occurred. It was no secret that as every new school year began, the Central Office set out its latest brainstorming, begotten while others were vacationing over the summer months. I must confess, also, that she may not have been properly informed that it was in the Fall season that the Jewish holidays kept me absent on scattered days.

When Mary Reid conferred with my troubled school principal and me, she carefully crafted an outline of all the advantages of the Central Office innovations. Her masterful performance had such a calming effect on the principal, that it would have been worthwhile as a video demonstration of how to handle complaints and criticism. I am certain she played a large role in the fine relationship which developed between this principal and me, which I enjoyed for the entire school year.

For the first day of school, Mary had scheduled each of her "pupil personnel workers" to be at one of their assigned schools. They were to serve as aides to the regular staff in acclimating students on the first day of the new school year. On that day, as I walked up the path to my newly assigned school – which was totally non-white – a little third or fourth grade girl looked at me with gleeful anticipation and asked, "Are you a new teacher?" As I shook my head "No," she responded with a long "Awww!" I couldn't have been more pleased, as it illustrated for me, as many times before and after, that my white skin was of little importance to African American children of all ages.

I found myself stimulated by my new circumstances in the region, and participated in two projects that year. One of them was totally of my own device. Stress management and "burn out" were topics much discussed in the literature of mental health providers during those years, and I observed that the problem was rampant among my colleagues. Yet, searching the local colleges, I could not discover any course being given on this topic. Thus, I decided to organize a four-session course, and engaged a professor from Johns Hopkins University, Dr. Lee Richardson, to lead it. She had published widely on the topic and was well recommended. A couple of my colleagues helped me with the publicity, registration, and collection of tuition, and school psychologists from other districts of Maryland were invited to attend. It took place in a large conference room at the regional office, and was well attended.

I was particularly pleased that the Region Five director thought enough of the idea that she sent a check written from her own personal account, enrolling one of her troubled school principals. After the first session, one of my colleagues told me that it was already worth the tuition.

Another project in which I participated was an innovation of Mary Reid's, that of forming a committee to explore needs of the schools. Five of us volunteered to serve on her committee; three psychologists, and two social workers. We drew up a questionnaire for school principals in the region, polling their needs in relation to problems of any nature, such as staffing, tardiness, student violence, vandalism, etc.

This survey resulted in some findings which I felt were too significant to ignore. I decided to write a description of the entire project, include a photograph of the members of the committee, and to submit it to *Communique´*, the monthly publication of the National Association of School Psychologists. I had been deriving much pleasure reading this periodical from cover to cover, ever since my entry into the school system. It was to be my first article in the *Communique´* and proved to be the beginning of a love affair with writing for them. I was particularly proud when this, my first article submitted, was accepted, inasmuch as in those early days almost all of the contributors were professors at distinguished universities.

Sadly for me and many others, Mary Reid had planned her retirement for the end of that school year. It seemed that the change from decentralization to centralization was in the works for Baltimore, as for many large school systems around the country. Thus, her position as regional director of pupil services workers was beginning to be phased out.

For the next year, although we were still to be stationed in the regional locations, someone from our ranks would be in charge, but with no elevation in status. It was the decision of Mrs. Reid as to whom this role was to be given for the following year. At my final conference with her, she kept asking me if I was interested in a supervisory role, without questioning directly if I wanted to do this. I consistently replied "No!", because I enjoyed working directly with the students too much to warrant any interruption.

I was not to see Mary Reid again until a couple of years later, when I chanced to meet her in a supermarket. I was delighted to see her. As we chatted, she told me of one of my colleagues, a woman who had been experiencing some difficult times. Her severe emotional problems had interfered with her ability to remain on medication, to function appropriately, and to care for her own needs. She had become, in effect, a street person, often sleeping in her auto. I guess I should not have been surprised that Mary, with her innate kindness, had provided this former employee with overnight lodging on several tight occasions.

It was typical of Mary Reid not to let race, color or creed interfere with doing the right and kind thing. Following that meeting in the supermarket, she and I remained in contact, and it was my good fortune over the years to continue hearing her words of wisdom and cheerful encouragement.

CHAPTER FOURTEEN

Jumping the Hurdles

Men make mistakes not because they think they know when they do not know but because they think others do not know.

Shalom Aleichem

The next year Lori Wizda, one of my fellow school psychologists, was named as interim head of Region Five pupil personnel workers. Although she did a fine job, and was supportive to me, no one could have replaced Mary Reid.

That year I was assigned a new elementary school, one which was attached to the building where the regional office was located. There were conveniences in having my school and regional office in attached buildings. However, two major events took place at that school, and one of them proved to be extremely vexing, turning into a stressful situation which was to last for almost the entire school year.

Early in the year, a four-year-old pre-school child named Jacob was referred to me by his teacher, because of his inability to remain seated, follow directions, or focus on any one task. The only way in which she could handle this child was if his mother remained in class, and unfortunately the mother's means of control consisted of keeping a threatening belt in view. Even though I don't think the mother actually struck the child in the classroom, the teacher – an affable, caring, and capable-appearing young woman – was appalled by the entire situation. Most of all his disruptions were such that they interfered with her management of the entire pre-school class.

I agreed that Jacob would benefit from a psychological evaluation in order to determine his functioning level and whatever factors might have led to his misbehavior. As his teacher was so troubled by his daily disruptions to her classroom, I agreed to make his case a priority.

Since there is usually little information available for a child so young, I was pleased to learn that the school nurse did have a folder of background material. However, when I approached the nurse for permission to see her folder, she held it high to her chest, and said, "This is confidential, private information! I cannot share it with you." This had never happened to me before, and I was really stunned. I then pleaded: "I need to examine every bit of information. You are blocking a crucial part of my evaluation!" She would not budge, repeating again, "No, you cannot see this folder!" The situation turned angrier and she and I were not very happy with each other to say the least. I learned later that the folder contained the records of an older sister who had been placed in foster care by protective services. In fairness to the nurse, I suppose she felt she was doing her best to protect the boy.

Physically, Jacob was a handsome, normal-appearing child. On the day that I evaluated him, he left the classroom with me eagerly enough, but once in my room, his behavior was exactly as it was in the classroom. He couldn't remain seated and appeared to be totally unfocussed as he wandered around my room. If I had not already had extensive experience evaluating hundreds of four-year-olds, I might not have been as certain of my conclusions concerning his significant intellectual deficits. Moreover, I was thinking to myself that I didn't need to go to graduate school to recognize a child so similar to my own disabled child, Michael.

The results of the testing revealed an IQ within the lower limits of the moderate range of intellectual limitation. When I revealed this to Jacob's teacher, telling her that he would be eligible for a special small class for disabled children, she was relieved. As part of my usual procedure with a child with intellectual limitations, I had a conference with Jacob's mother to counsel and prepare her – in my most gentle manner – for the results that I would be reporting at a team meeting. However, when I did report my findings, all sorts of unforeseen and upsetting events took place.

Seated at the meeting with me were the speech pathologist who conducted the meeting, the parent (with Jacob sitting quietly on her lap), the reading resource teacher, the hitherto uncommunicative school nurse, and another woman whom I had never met before. This new person turned out to be one of the special education supervisors assigned to the regional office, which was conveniently located in the adjoining building. I soon realized she was present at the invitation of the nurse, to serve as a backup to help her to deal with any difficulties she might have with my report.

When called on to report on my findings, I related that Jacob's intellectual functioning was significantly below average, with a label of "moderate mental retardation." The nurse and her friend both looked at Jacob – who sat on his mother's lap appearing as normal as could be – and both shook their heads "No! This can't be!" One of them declared: "We will need a second opinion!" Their response was an entirely new experience for me, and I am happy to say it was the only time in my tenure as a school psychologist that something like it ever occurred. I was left quite speechless.

Inasmuch as this all took place before strict federal guidelines and time lines were in place, these two women had the power to put the entire process on hold until they arranged for another evaluation. Needless to say, I was baffled and frustrated over this needless blockage of help for a handicapped child. The other team members and the classroom teacher were all totally sympathetic and supportive of my plight, but all they could do was to sit back and wait to see what would happen.

I consulted with my supervisor, Dr. Michael Oidick, and while supportive of my position, he too said there was nothing we could do but sit back and wait. As it happened, the two ladies arranged for a series of evaluations with outside speech pathologists, psychologists, special educators, and physical therapists. It all took many, many months, and it wasn't until the final evaluation at the Kennedy Institute in late spring that all the findings were in.

Much to the surprise of the ladies, the results indicated that Jacob was not within the low moderate range, but even lower than that, and was described as "profoundly retarded."

During these many months I had absented myself from attending further team meetings, unable and unwilling to sit at the table with these women. Jacob's teacher and the other sympathetic team members kept me informed of all the evaluations. After the results were in, there was not a word of formal acknowledgment or a semblance of apology for me from either of my erstwhile opponents.

However, justice often finds a path in strange ways, and one never knows what good things lie ahead. In future years, both of these women were to demonstrate their remorse for doubting my findings and delaying help for Jacob. We were destined to meet in other schools on other teams.

They would prove to display great appreciation for my skills as a school psychologist, and to extend themselves through numerous acts of friendship.

As divine justice would have it, the nurse, a couple of years later, was on the team at two of the middle schools where I was assigned. How I cringed when I first learned of her presence but I was soon to change my attitude. Without saying any words, she exhibited respect for any opinion I may have had expressed in discussing a child, and always sided with my view in any team conflicts. But the greatest honor she was to pay me took place one summer while I was out of the country. When I returned, she called and told me she had tried for so long to reach me and was disappointed that she was unable to locate me. I was amazed when I learned that she wished to engage me privately to evaluate her own grandchild.

At another time in the future, the nurse's accomplice, formerly a supervisor from the regional office, was also assigned to one of my elementary schools. Her position had changed, and she was now a traveling team manager with whom I would be working one day each week.

When I first learned that she would be my team manager, my response was "Oh no! No way I will be able to work with her!" But again, I had forgotten how things always change.

To my astonishment, she appeared as friendly as could be. Although it was her manner to respond to many people with highly critical comments, impatience, and rudeness, she was always respectful towards me to the point of being embarrassing! In fact, one day one of the team members declared, out of her hearing, "No matter what Mrs. Blumberg says about a child, the manager always takes her view!" I could only smile to myself. On another occasion, I jokingly lamented that my pencils were always so short, because no one ever gave me any supplies. At the next meeting, she presented me with two packs of new pencils.

Returning to the tale of my elementary school, another event of a more significant nature took place. The principal invited me to present a half-day workshop to her staff, as part of the mid-year staff development program. As a school administrator, her greatest concerns were the noise level in general, and the disruptive behaviors of many of her students. Thus she welcomed my topic, which I had labeled "A Mini-Course in Behavior Management." I felt confident and sufficiently prepared with my illustrated overhead projections, comprehensive handouts, and planned group participation activities, and it was very well received by the staff. One of my young fellow psychologists, on learning of my program, visited my school to attend. She paid me the highest complement, by declaring afterward, "You're a real pro!"

It was over a week later that I had a brief conference with the principal, and I couldn't have been more delighted with her praise. She said that "In terms of the noise level, the first day after your presentation it was a little quieter." Then, proceeding slowly, she continued, "Actually, each day afterward, the noise level diminished a bit more! By the end of the week our school was satisfactorily quiet."

Nevertheless, in this same conference, she went on to add some sharp words of criticism: "I do feel, however, that you have over-reacted with the problem case of Jacob. It seems a person with your skills and psychological tools should have been able to handle the matter with less anger!"

She was referring to the fact that I had absented myself from the team meetings for almost the entire year. And of course, she was absolutely right! Her remonstration planted a seed in my mind that perhaps I could benefit by learning to reduce my over-sensitivity to criticism.

The truth of the matter is that my years with Title I had given me little experience in working with teams. Great as my gratification was with working with teachers, parents, and especially the children, I was never really comfortable at team meetings. It would take more time and other hurdles before I conquered this weakness and became a "pro" who was also in total control at a meeting. It would be a while yet before I became a professional team member whose words were listened to by all with respectful deference.

CHAPTER FIFTEEN

Things Go Topsy Turvy for the Psychologists

How great some men would be were they not arrogant.
Talmud Tractate Kallah Rabbathi 3

The next year, the inevitable changes that take place in September as the schools open, wrought havoc for all of the school psychologists. The major switch was from decentralization, with several regional offices located throughout the city, to centralization. All of the regional offices were closed, and so all of the special education service providers were suddenly in the domain of the Central Office.

That year a new person, solicited from another large city, had a major role in planning for the psychologists. Having little knowledge of the complexities of our professional responsibilities, she began by restructuring our work load. Her brainstorm was to divide all of the psychologists into two groups. One half would be assigned to traveling teams which were to spend all of their days attending team meetings, covering all of the schools in the city. The other half were designated to be the evaluators, each serving as many as ten schools, testing those children approved by the teams.

Fortunately, I was one of those selected to do evaluations, and at first I was as shaken by this turn of events and the drastic change in my work schedule, as were all the other psychologists. However, with my proclivity at that time to avoid school team meetings, I realized that this lottery-like selection of me as an evaluator was the lesser of two evils. There were others who disliked testing, and who were satisfied with their lot as floating team members.

In any event, the die was cast, and there was nothing anyone could do to change the "evil edict" for that year. I was shown a list of schools by Dr. Oidick and told I could select any ten I preferred. Naturally I quickly chose those closest to my home, even though I knew nothing about most of them.

For a number of reasons, it turned out to be a pleasant and productive year of growth for me. As there were not enough people evaluating, there were long waiting lists at each school where I served. When I arrived at any of my newly assigned schools, I was welcomed by all with open arms, and hugged by any staff members who knew me from other years. I was given choice locations in which to work in the schools, and the administrators eagerly delivered the children to me, often even before I could take off my coat and set up my materials.

In terms of my responsibilities, the list was short. I was merely being asked to test the child and to write and submit a report. There were no meetings, no lists of children to counsel, no scheduled appointments with parents and staff members. However, I set my own rigid standards, and it was not unusual for my work day to end far later than it should have. As usual, I lunched as I worked.

It had always been my dictum that each parent was entitled to a private conference with the psychologist who evaluated their child. Because I was not able to share my findings with any team, in deference to the floating crew, I made it my business to have a private conference with each parent and to share any pertinent information with teachers or administrators. I followed up on my recommendations, and was diligent with referring those with suspected or untreated medical problems to outside agencies.

With the repetitious use of the Wechsler, the most important intelligence test we used, my skills and speed were perfected. After a while I became as proficient with the Wechsler as I was with the Binet from earlier years. It was always my feeling that the more quickly the actual testing, the more time I could devote to interviewing the child and fostering growth in his or her self-concept. Working quickly often also led to a child's wish to stay with me longer, and to ask, "When will I see you again?" or, "Will I be seeing you every week?"

In the formal testing, if there were eleven subtests to be administered, I devised a practical way to eliminate a minute of time from each, through more efficient handling of the materials. I began to memorize the exact wording of the questions and the correct answers, wasting no time and promoting a maximum of eye contact. I reorganized my manual with marker tabs for each subtest, allowing me to flip through the pages with lightening speed. I lined up the numerous testing pieces in the kit and on my testing table almost obsessively. However, this all permitted me to present the cumbersome pieces of materials with rapid, invisible movements.

I concentrated, too, on improving my report writing. It had always been my concern that lay people find all psychological reports hard to understand. As it is with any profession, it is difficult to explain complex concepts in simple terms. So I took as many terms as I could – mostly those which sound to others like "gobbledy gook" – and explored other ways to express them. Also, I expanded and simplified recommendations for parents and teachers. Always, I found something positive to put in my report about every child I saw, regardless of how limited or badly behaved the student may have appeared. I was to reap benefits from all of these enhancements of my report writing for the remainder of my career.

My days were filled with contentment until one fateful day. On this particular day, I saw an unusual child, one with three challenging disabilities. Among them were an already diagnosed visual impairment, a learning disability, and a form of elective mutism. That is, she would not ever speak to the teacher, or to other students while in class. I called her mother immediately after seeing her, and fortunately she was available to confer with me that very afternoon, albeit keeping me at the school overtime. I arrived home late and exhausted, ready to tell my husband of my grueling day. Alas, I was greeted at home by a personal letter from someone at the Central Office, the very lady who divided all the psychologists in the two groups, designating me as a "tester." In her letter, she requested that I call her office immediately to schedule an appointment, in view of my "low productivity." I read the letter with disbelief, thinking it must be some kind of error.

I immediately called the supervisor of city-wide psychologists, Dr. Oidick, who confirmed that many such letters had gone out from the office of this newly hired administrator. He was highly sympathetic and told me not worry, that he would support me personally by joining me whenever I met with her.

Before meeting with her, I spoke to some of the other evaluators. One of them – who had been on sick leave for two months following major surgery – had also received such a letter! Her first reaction upon receiving this insult was that it was a prank being played on her by an insensitive colleague. At this point, the entire matter might have become hilarious but, there was a real fear that the words, "Low Productivity" could become part of a permanent file in the central office.

Before the meeting took place I took the time to respond in writing, defending myself. I enclosed some of the articles that I had published, and explained my activities at my school on that same fateful day. Some excerpts from my letter follow:

Last Friday I was assigned to evaluate a six-year-old girl who experiences visual deficits and a learning disability, along with suspected emotional problems. It was quite a complex case, as well as urgent, and required two phone conferences with outside agencies, an interview with the parent, and a total of five conferences with the administrator, classroom teacher, speech clinician and vision teacher. This was all in addition to observing the child in the classroom, evaluating her and completing the report. Because of the urgency of the case, I worked as I ate my bag lunch. When I arrived home late that day, I was dismayed at your letter describing me in terms of "low productivity." I did not know whether to laugh or cry.

On the day of my appointment, Dr. Oidick faithfully kept his word supporting me with his presence. At this meeting, not a word was spoken by her of her foolish letter to me. Instead, she gave a friendly, gentle speech about lofty, abstract goals for students, those goals shared by her and the Baltimore City Public Schools. If she was embarrassed by the entire matter, she certainly knew how to disguise it. Excerpts from a letter from her, closing the matter follow:

By way of this letter I am directing the office of psychological services to destroy the copy of my letter criticizing your productivity level, as we will do from our office files. Please accept my best regards for your continued success as you continue to provide such a valuable service to students of Baltimore City.

Digressing ahead, I enjoyed much applause in future years resulting from my efforts that year with refining my written psychological reports. When colleagues from other disciplines whom I had never met, read my reports, it was not unusual for them to note my name and to offer compliments when they met me. Also, it was not unusual for them to single me out on the basis of my reports, to refer special clients to me, saying "I know from reading your reports that I want you to evaluate this child."

The greatest compliment of all however, came from a pediatrician who had never met me. One day she called a mutual friend, asking, "Who is Thelma Alpert Blumberg?" She then explained to my friend that she had served as a volunteer at team meetings at Bais Yaakov, a non-public Jewish school. In the course of doing this, she had recently spent an entire day there, reading psychological reports. Her comment to my friend was, "Thelma Alpert Blumberg's reports were the only ones which were written in language that I could understand."

Thus, my "topsy turvy" year turned into a genuinely productive one, one I am glad I didn't miss. As proven again and again, difficult, painful times can reap huge returns. Unseen, as in the underside of a beautiful tapestry, the weaving of the fabric conceals the mysteries and beauty of life.

CHAPTER SIXTEEN

All Good Things

Pleasant words are as a honey comb, sweet to the soul, and health to the bones.

Book of Proverbs 1:24

That year of solitary testing proved to be productive despite the foolishness meted out by the lady at the Central Office, but it was still a great relief when the next year arrived and the work load for the school psychologists returned to a relatively normal state. Staff members at my schools were particularly pleased that their support people were back to their old roles, and that they could count on seeing them on a weekly basis. I was made to feel welcome by everyone at all of my schools.

On the other hand, the warm reception I received may have been mere feelings of relief for the restoration of normal services. Perhaps my genuine interest in the students was recognized, or maybe it was that people began noticing my "grindstone" habits and my apparent lack of concern when working overtime or through lunch. Or, it could have been that the body of my writing and publications, which grew each year, provided me with some "fame." In any event, it was a period of relative calm during which a great many good things happened, all in my favor.

Teams were composed mostly of school-based staff members, and in most schools the reading resource teacher, and occasionally a speech pathologist would serve as the team managers. All of the special service providers attended the weekly meetings, at which time problems and special placement of individual students were discussed. Even though there was a kind of pecking order among some members, the meetings also served as a cementing social feature for the support staff. It gave me special satisfaction that my guidance was beginning to be valued, sought after, and surprisingly followed with near-reverence.

In the early eighties the Central Office was still adjusting to the new federal law, PL 94-142, passed in the seventies. Suddenly it was necessary that the file of each special education student evaluated by a speech pathologist contain a signed written report by the school psychologist.

To make this possible, during the summer months while others were vacationing, one of those special groups at the Central Office had devised a speedy way to supply the folder of each special education student with a report by a school psychologist. A report called a "Cognitive Assessment" was being requested for hundreds of children who were considered "out of compliance," and so it was now deemed acceptable for the school psychologist to do a "write off" on a report of an evaluation administered by a speech pathologist. School psychologists were being asked to write a report using the test results of the speech pathologists, for children we may have never met.

Although there was much resistance from all of the psychologists on ethical grounds, for a couple of years it remained as a Central Office "dictum" which needed to be followed.

Fortunately I found an ethical way of fulfilling the new rules. Most speech pathologists in those days used a test called the "Detroit Test of Language Ability." I knew that this measure was really an intelligence test, and a quite good one, used by the speech people for testing language. Therefore, I used their results from this Detroit Test, converting the information into the intellectual values measured and described by school psychologists. As I could be quite comfortable dashing off large numbers of these reports each day, I was treasured at all of my schools for keeping their records in compliance.

Another feature which was helpful to me resulted from my published writing. It was my genuine belief that there was no more interesting place to be spending my days than in the public schools. Because so many engrossing incidents occurred each day, I was filled with the desire to describe them in writing. Thus, I practically leaped with joy when I read that the Maryland State Association of School Psychologists (MSPA) was conducting a "Case Study" contest. I quickly entered a brief description of one of my students with whom I had enjoyed so much success. Even though this particular story went back to my very first year at work, it was one of my favorites, and I titled it, "The Boy Who Wanted to Sweep the Halls." Lo and behold, I was the winner of the contest!

I was awarded the prize at the fall convention of the Maryland School Psychologist Association. Following that, the Baltimore Sun, the largest newspaper in Baltimore, printed a large feature article describing the state meeting and the status and growth of school psychology. I was interviewed for the article by a Sun reporter, and my case study became the focus of the newspaper feature. The article created a great stir among the staff in one of my middle schools. They were enthralled with "their" school psychologist being featured. Nevertheless, it was fortunate that this glory was short-lived, because for a couple of weeks I was so besieged by phone calls from parents and requests from staff members, that it interfered with my regular responsibilities. Here we have an example of the corollary to our basic premise: "Sometimes bad things come from good!"

During that same period, I branched out into another direction, that of organizing and moderating a panel discussion for the Baltimore Association of School Psychologists (BCASP). The new Federal Law had a clause stating that parents must be present at all meetings concerning their children, and this had become a new concern for some of the school psychologists. Because of my experiences with my own son, I had an awareness of their common misperceptions about parents of special children and I felt that many of the school psychologists would benefit from more knowledge about the unique needs of the parents of such children.

I therefore organized a panel for BCASP members – a panel of four very special parents of handicapped children. Each parent held an important position within a school system. Besides myself, my panel included two school Principals who were the parents of intellectually limited children, and two teacher specialists, one whose son had a hearing impairment, and another whose daughter had a vision handicap.

When I informed the BCASP committee of my panel plan, they were highly enthusiastic. However, I told them that I had no experience as a moderator, and would not know how to handle that part of the program. In the course of thinking it over, however, I realized how foolish it was to delegate my own program to another, and to my own surprise, I became the moderator! As it happened, in the midst of introducing the panelists in opening the program, I could see my friend Gail Levy sitting in the center of the packed audience, and I was spurred on by her when her lips mouthed to me, "Very Good!"

My writing career expanded in all ways. I branched out to reporting my school exploits to respected counseling journals, in addition to the National and Maryland State psychological publications. Little did I dream that at a later date, when computers became common and I would be able to write so much more quickly, I would be invited to serve as a Contributing Editor for the *Communique´*, the excellent monthly publication of the National Association of School Psychologists.

I derived great satisfaction at that early time when the newsletter of the Maryland School Psychological Association described my writing in the national media with this special announcement:

"BE ON THE WATCH: Thelma Alpert Blumberg WRITES AGAIN!"

Yet, despite all of the good things of that period, there would still lay ahead an as-yet undreamed of humiliation....

CHAPTER SEVENTEEN

Bullied Again: I Learn the Ropes

*Your friend has a friend, and your friend's friend
has a friend (so be discreet).*
Talmud Tractate Kethuboth 109b

It was true that from the very beginning of my career I enjoyed outstanding success working with individual students, teachers, and parents. Yet, I would have given myself failing grades when it came to handling groups at team meetings. Somehow, echoing down from my childhood, my innate shyness played a role.

The adult bully, like the child, knows its prey. Professionals who respond quickly in a group, whether right or wrong, tend to command respect. Thus, less informed but more pushy, verbal members of a team could "upstage" me and steal my clout, and a time came when I actually experienced the most devastating of blows at the hands of two bullies.

However, as from all painful experiences, I gained that year in ways which forevermore protected me from being trampled on again.

At one school, two disturbing events occurred, both involving conflict at team meetings. When Baltimore City Schools continued having difficulty meeting federal requirements for servicing their handicapped students, changes were made by the Central Office. To improve uniformity, they devised a plan whereby the school-based managers were replaced by traveling team managers.

There were pitfalls with this new plan. These traveling managers visited each school either weekly, every other week, or even two half-days a month, depending on the size of the school and how many cases needed to be discussed for special education. It was often difficult for the managers to achieve union with the team already set at the school, and all of this paved the road for animosities between the new managers and the school-based people.

Thus, at one of my schools, the wheels were in motion for an explosion. The visiting manager there was a very capable, well groomed, youngish man, but at the same time, proved to be offensively controlling. Because of this, a clash erupted between him and the previously compatible team, including me. This eruption became the most distressing of all staff conflicts I had ever experienced.

The traveling manager at my once-happy school managed to offend everyone on the team. Each week he would upset the assistant principal, a dear gentle lady, demanding that she bring him all types of supplies such as a stapler, paper clips, and folders. It took many visits until he began to carry some supplies with him. With banal clumsiness, he managed to make every petty matter into a declaration of war. Most serious of all, he treated all the members of the team as his underlings in crucial matters concerning the children, expecting them to follow all his decisions regarding controversial labeling.

The first of two serious flareups which concerned me involved the question of which features must be necessary to label a child "Learning Disabled." With new directions written into the Federal Law, this became an issue which plagued teams at schools around the country. Different states interpreted the law differently, and even neighboring districts in each state did not always agree. Our problem was whether to use actual IQ scores and standard scores of educational assessments as cutoff points, or to bring clinical judgment into the picture. The decision became a crucial one because only those children who were labeled "Learning Disabled" were eligible for special education services. Furthermore, in terms of background training and a thorough understanding required, this topic was really the domain of the school psychologist.

One case became particularly sticky. After evaluating a young boy and studying all the factors involved, I had determined that he indeed qualified as learning disabled, even though his scores didn't quite match the magic formula set up by our district. Our rigid, "nit picking" manager couldn't function beyond the numbers on his chart, and disagreed with me. This was a child whom I felt would benefit from special services, and I could not budge from my position. The disagreement seemed unsolvable at the school level so one of the administrators suggested that we call in the manager's supervisor, along with Dr. Oidick, my supervisor from the Central Office. Upon examining the information, Dr. Oidick agreed with my position, and to my relief, told me that there was no need for him to come to the meeting. The manager's supervisor did attend, and she too agreed with me, settling that matter.

With my sensitivity such as it was – with my back up, so to speak – this entire case provided me many days of anguish, despite an outcome in my favor. I had won the battle, but seemed likely to lose the war.

The outcome of the second conflict with our manager proved to be the most devastating of all. Each of the team members had experiences of his own with the manager, similar to mine, and were beginning to feel very uncomfortable on the days when he was with us. It was largely a matter of his overbearing and abrasive manner, and indifference to the feelings of his colleagues. Two of them came to me, pleading for help. They reasoned that, as I was a traveling team member also, serving other schools, I was in a better position than they to improve the situation. Not thinking this through carefully enough, I foolishly agreed to approach the principal with our problem. The team was elated and relieved.

There were, however, two crucial factors that I did not fully realize at the time. The principal, a tall, attractive, sharp-tongued woman, could be unpredictable, and had a history of intimidating many of her own staff members. When I approached her, telling her about the anguish of her two staff members, she seemed conciliatory and supportive. She suggested that we all meet with her and the manager. Another critical fact which I didn't realize at that time was that this attractive principal and the well groomed manager had friendly "professional" connections outside of the school. They both taught an evening class at the same community college, and both attended regular gatherings of the same social group.

The meeting turned out to be a most astonishing and bizarre event. The principal opened up by changing the agenda in such a way that it took a while for all of us to realize what was happening. What she did was to turn the focus of the entire problem directly at me! When she forbade her staff to discuss cases with me outside of the meetings, I sat there in shock. The only one who spoke up was my loyal supporter, the assistant principal, who kept interrupting and protesting this attack on me. My two friends on whose behalf I had spoken to the principal in the first place, remained too terrified to say a word.

Needless to say, I was devastated by this meeting. Although this had always been a favorite school, my thoughts turned to transferring for the coming year. However, I made a wise decision – it was not a good idea to leave any school in haste and anger.

Immediately afterward, one of the team members who was silent at the meeting met with me and apologized for what had happened. I knew she really regretted the unpredicted outcome. The other silent team member followed the principal's directive and stopped speaking to me. Since she always had been an admirer of mine, I cornered her one day when no one was present. I was unprepared for her emotional response – she lowered her head to her folded arms on the table, and broke into a fit of sobbing.

I wondered if at the end of the year the principal might request that a different school psychologist replace me. However, our unpredictable principal surprised me again! In my mail box in June was a copy of an evaluation of my work sent to Lois Thomas, Supervisor of all Support Services at the Central Office. It read as follows:

In response to your request for information
regarding the quality of psychological services
provided by Thelma Alpert Blumberg at my school, I offer
the following remarks:
She is very thorough in all of her psychological
assessments and is particularly adept in explaining
test results to parents and staff at screening
meetings.
Mrs. Blumberg is extremely knowledgeable about
the field of child psychology and constantly
seeks to increase her expertise.
In conclusion, I can always count on Mrs.
Blumberg to "go the extra mile" as we at the
school level work to find the most appropriate
placement for our students. She is definitely
an asset to our school's educational program.

I remained at that favorite school of mine for many years afterward, long after that "charming" lady left, working contentedly with a number of outstanding and successful principals.

In any event, there were three lessons learned from this experience which I was able to pass on to younger colleagues and to clients over the coming years:

The first rule is "Never complain to a supervisor about the behavior of a colleague." (That is, unless their behavior involves danger to anyone.)

The second was that whenever involved in any conflict involving peers within any organization, "It is always best to refrain from critical gossip about colleagues." The fact that one can never know of the alliances and friendships of those with whom you share the gossip is just one reason, among many, for this dogma. Of course avoidance of "evil gossip" is a well-known dictum among those who observe the Jewish faith.

The third rule and perhaps the most important was, "Regardless of how upsetting a situation with others may seem, do not overreact."

Not too long after my fiasco with the principal and manager, I received an invitation in the mail to attend a one-day conference on the topic "Improving Self-Concept for Professional Women." This grabbed my attention immediately, and it was fortunate I enrolled. The conference took place in a large Baltimore hotel. A dynamic speaker of national fame presided over an audience of hundreds of professional women. I was to learn many things in that one day which would be extremely helpful for my entire career.

One of the topics covered was "Getting along with difficult people." This was my first exposure to new literature classifying difficult people into types, and providing strategies for living with them. In that one day I learned about significant responses which I could apply immediately when needed. Brief, simplified examples of ways to respond to critics were demonstrated, such as: displaying empathy by finding out exactly what the critic means, avoiding being judgmental or defensive, finding some way to agree with the critic, and explaining your position tactfully and assertively.

I was amazed to learn that I was not alone among professional men and women who responded with overblown sensitivity to bullies and their unkind behavior in the workplace. The presenter described the situation of a high-ranking corporate manager whom she had counseled. While her client was sitting at a board meeting offering a suggestion, one of his colleagues cut him short and ridiculed his comments. He was so distressed that he had to excuse himself immediately, driven to tears by such a blow to his ego. Although I had observed numerous co-workers driven to tears, publicly, I was pleased to realize that this had never happened to me. All in all I learned new responses at the conference which immediately changed the course of my behavior at team meetings. Colleagues could no longer tread on my feet!

There was one additional bit of advice given by the presenter. She stressed the importance of not skipping lunch, but instead, advised lunching with colleagues. I found this amusing inasmuch as my driven inclination to put the needs of the children first made me a chronic failure in taking time for lunch. However, it did give me much food for thought....

At about that same time a new book appeared on library shelves, titled, "Feeling Good." It was written by Dr. David Burns, a University of Pennsylvania psychology professor. The book discussed practical uses of cognitive therapy, and it inspired me to read everything I could on the topic. Dr. Burns labeled ten misperceptions held by many people regarding their interactions with others and he spelled out clear ways to correct these errors. His advice for dealing with difficult people was detailed, practical, and easy to apply. It was a treatment with which I was so comfortable that I felt that I would soon be prepared to deliver workshops on the topic myself.

With my new skills I would no longer have to give myself failing grades when it came to handling groups at team meetings. Instead, my major crisis of that year proved to be a crossroads in my maturation. I was never again to ring alarm bells in the face of a victimizing bully.

CHAPTER EIGHTEEN

Surprising New Clients

*Man must not rely on pure reason; he must mix faith
with it.*

Rabbi Nachman of Bratslav, Leo Rosten

Ever since my entry into the Baltimore City Public Schools, I felt that
there was no more fascinating or absorbing way to spend my days. Yet,
when a new population of parents and their offspring was added to my
case load at a Northwest Baltimore school, the enchantments as well as
demands grew geometrically. These new clients were families served by
the Orthodox Jewish Day Schools.

As part of the new Public Law 94-142, enacted in 1975, children
with handicaps who attended non-public schools were mandated to
receive some special education services at their zoned public school. As
it happened, one of my assigned schools in Northwest Baltimore was the
zoned school for a number of these families. Thus, in the early 1980's
we began to receive referrals at my school for a few of these Jewish
children who attended non-public schools. At the same time the schools
in Northeast Baltimore received referrals from their zoned non-public
school children, mostly Catholic, who lived there.

All of our new clients from Jewish private schools were part of
a distinctive religious culture, all following the rules of the Jewish
Sabbath, where no work is performed from Friday sunset until Saturday
sunset. Primarily, the Sabbath is set aside solely as a means for family
togetherness and spiritual renewal, with prayer, study, singing, festive
meals, and gatherings with friends. The girls dress modestly, with skirts
falling below the knee, regardless of the current fashion. The boys all
wear "skull caps," as a reminder that their Creator is above them. Many of
the homes do not have television and those which do often keep the set in
a closet, for select viewing. At the same time, the walls of these homes are
usually stacked with books dealing with Jewish religion and philosophy.

Previous to passage of the new law, all of these cases were handled by a team from the Central Office, and evaluations were meted out to psychologists at any number of different schools. Over the years I had been hearing firsthand reports from some of my colleagues, bemoaning these cases as unwelcome burdens. In fact, I had read reports from outside clinics, with detailed, critical descriptions of these families! As a Sabbath observer myself, it would offend me to hear the disparaging remarks about these parents and their children, their unusual customs, and the "odd" dress which some of them wore.

When responsibility for this new population was shifted to my school, there was some resistance there too from staff members. Part of this was justified, inasmuch as it was not until many years later that additional staff were engaged to handle the overflow. In the early days, it meant squeezing more clients into the already-crowded workload of our team.

Understandably, there were many adjustments for me and my colleagues in handling this population. Indeed, as I conferred privately with the mother of the first of these children, I was unexpectedly summoned by the assistant principal to attend a meeting in another room. I realized quickly that I was not scheduled or needed at the other meeting. What really happened was that the assistant principal, an otherwise kindly and supportive colleague, felt threatened that I took valuable school time to confer with a parent from a non-public school.

There were other hurdles, too. I cringed once at a team meeting when one of my team members berated a parent for depriving her children of a television set. Another, a team manager, would uncaringly keep the parents waiting for their scheduled appointments, saying, "They can wait!" Some team members could not understand why any of the less affluent of these parents would burden themselves with the expenses of a private school. I would find myself explaining that the primary motivation was not exclusiveness, but rather, religious and ideological. I confided to my team members that those families who could not really afford the private school tuition received scholarships from solicited charitable donations.

I must admit that I found working with these children distinctive. Their Hebrew names such as Yedida or Shulamit, all appeared unpronounceable. When interviewed, they sometimes used Hebrew or Yiddish terms such as tzedeka, (charity), Shabbas, (Sabbath), or daven, (prayer). It helped that I have a limited knowledge of Hebrew and could pronounce their names correctly, and that I usually understood what they were saying.

The pictures which they drew often included boys with the skull caps (yarmulkes) and the fringes (tsitsis) that they wore. Their responses could be unusual and quotable. For example, I once heard a comical reply while administering the old WISC-R (a basic intelligence test) to a seven-year-old boy. When presented with a picture of a cow from the picture completion subtest – a picture which deliberately omitted the line representing a split hoof –he blurted out, "That's not a kosher cow!" I knew immediately he was referring to the biblical injunction that only a cow with a split hoof can be kosher.

Parents too could be amusing. One parent listened thoughtfully to my carefully considered description of her child's intellectual strengths and weaknesses. In my usual manner I guardedly avoided any offensive terms. When I finished I asked if she had any questions. She then inquired quite innocently, "What ever happened to old-fashioned dumb?"

Among the children and families with whom I worked, there was one who was most unforgettable. His mother was an administrator in the special education division at the Baltimore County Schools. Consequently, she understood the Federal and State guidelines regarding special education, and realized that her troubled son could be eligible for counseling from our school psychologist. Unfortunately, the seven-year-old boy, Benjy, had severe behavior, attention, and emotional problems.

By age seven, he had already been suspended from two of the Jewish Day Schools, and was now being given a second chance at one of them. It seems he had bitten a teacher while in kindergarten, was physically aggressive with peers, and severely agitating to his parents and siblings. A school team agreed to offer him private counseling for one hour weekly. At that time, he was already being seen on a regular basis by an outside psychiatrist and was taking six prescribed medications.

Benjy was an attractive second grader, with curly, red hair. After my first meeting with him, I heard him tell his father, who picked him up, "Time went fast!" However, at successive meetings, over a period of weeks, I did not feel much success. I had set goals, based on his records, my own evaluations, and parent and teacher consultations, but it seemed that nothing was meeting with success. As he seemed so depressed and only minimally cooperative, I really wished to find some alternate treatment, or simply to rid myself of this case.

In one of my conferences with his mother, she urged me to phone his psychiatrist. Hesitantly, I called and confided my disappointment with making no progress with any of my goals. To my relief, he gave me some life-saving advice: forget my goals and "just think nourishment!"

One day, after the passage of a few weeks, Benjy began asking me some unexpected questions. He queried, "Do you see many other boys?" Following that he wanted to know how much time I spent with the other boys with whom I worked, and whether or not I liked them. It was then that he said the most surprising thing of all; he declared, "You know, you are the best doctor I have ever had!" Strangely enough, that simple praise from this second grade, seven-year-old boy, enabled me to continue, and to meet with gradual progress. Benjy was with me for two-and-a-half years and happily, a good many of my "goals" were realized.

At this time, my elementary school was temporarily located in a near-by middle school, due to massive remodeling. I was given a large health suite in the main building of this middle school for evaluating and counseling my clients, yet meetings were held at a portable building, an out-of-doors location at the far-end of the school property. After seeing my students in the health suite at 8:00 A.M., I had to rush to the portable building for the long day of meetings beginning at 9:00 A.M. I usually carried my testing equipment, my laptop, and my files for the day – just one example of the exhausting routine rush and pressure in performing my day's work!

I seemed to be well received by these Day School parents and their children. In fact, I was really flattered when an invitation came from one parent, who was also an administrator at one of the schools, to chair a session at a tri-state educational convention of the Jewish Day Schools. The topic he requested was "Understanding the Psychological Report." I resisted at first, hoping to persuade him to select another topic. Upon his insistence, I accepted, putting much effort into organizing slides, and preparing a structured lecture. It was received successfully, and I was able to present it afterward to a variety of different staff groups at the Baltimore City Schools.

I should add that a small number of these Day School students were from families who had recently emigrated to the United States from Iran, Russia, or Israel. Often the language in the homes of these children would be Iranian, Russian, or Hebrew. Thus the evaluation and planning for them was further complicated by the complexities accompanying any child with limited English proficiency, and for whom the common dangers of mislabeling apply.

It was always my feeling that children's learning and psychological problems do not vary much across different religions and cultures. Nonetheless, while it is certainly not necessary that a therapist be of the same race, religion, or culture, it is important for service providers to learn about and to be knowledgeable of their differences.

For example I had an experience which demonstrates such a lack of understanding. Within one week I had conferences with two parents of children whom I had evaluated. One was a well-educated, middle-class African American, while the other was an Orthodox Jewish woman. By coincidence, both parents had recently seen the same therapist at a nearby hospital. Both told me that the psychiatrist, who was from one of the Asian countries, did not understand their needs, and that she had offended them by her questions. Her approach to the African American mother was degrading, in that it suggested she viewed her as an educationally and socially deprived woman. At the same time, the Orthodox Jewish parent found the therapist's questions about sexual subjects rude and offensive. It was not difficult to see this was most likely a matter of lack of knowledge of cultural differences on the part of the foreign-born therapist.

I was extremely pleased to watch the entire non-public population at my school come to greatly value our professionalism. I credit all of this to the proficiency of two special team managers. One of them, Ann Bennett, who was the team manager at my school for many years, handled every task she undertook with compulsive exactness. There was never a lapse in her detailed handling of clients' cases, either in written form or in her sensitive handling of the needs of parents and children. It may have helped, too, that she was a Catholic who, herself, had attended the Catholic school system, from kindergarten through graduate school. She had an inherent knowledge of the intricacies of the non-public situation which she utilized to the advantage of all.

The other excellent manager, in charge at a later time, was Barbara Small, an African-American woman. By that time the number and population of the Jewish Day Schools in Baltimore had grown so much that their file folders took up an entire cabinet. Barbara Small shared with her predecessor, Ann Bennett, the same exactness with paper work, and an unstinting caring for the needs of children and their parents. Although she did not have the private schooling that Ann had, she was endowed with innate skills and abilities, which were outstanding. Under her tutelage, the highest level of professionalism persisted.

No Time for Lunch

It must be said that what could have been a permanent conflict between two groups of ill-matched cultures became, instead, a happy marriage.

CHAPTER NINETEEN

My Hidden Agenda: the Parents

He who does not support needy parents bears evil testimony against himself

Tana de Ben Eliahu

It was not unusual for any team member to have a hidden agenda, and I had mine. As the parent of a handicapped child myself, I had a special interest in every parent with whom I worked. I virtually sat at "both sides of the desk," and I felt an obligation to protect parents against any indifference or insensitivity which might occur.

It is true that the majority of staff and team members with whom I have worked did generally display sensitivity when dealing with parents. Yet, there were also a number of them who simply did not know how to relate to parents. I would cringe when I heard comments made privately about a child such as, "The apple doesn't fall far from the tree!" I once sat at a meeting where a teacher told a parent, again and again, that her son was "s-o-o low." A nurse at a team meeting once told a parent bluntly, "It is a waste of money to have your child tutored – it isn't helping!" I have heard people express disdain for working with all parents, and then wonder why they were having problems with them!

Perhaps my role as a parent overtook that of a professional, and I may have been guilty of harshness to these colleagues.

As it happened, my obsession with the needs of these "special parents" was such that, in the 1980s I wrote two important pieces on the topic. One appeared as a chapter in a book titled Related Services for Handicapped Children, (Esterson and Bluth, Eds.), published by Little, Brown and Co. The name of my chapter was "Parent Counseling and Training." Another, an article which appeared in *Communique´*, the monthly publication of the National Association of School Psychologists, was entitled, "Parents of Handicapped Children: Five Preconceived Myths."

In addition, I took particular pleasure in addressing parent groups, and teaching them strategies for improving behaviors. I enjoyed demonstrating to them that when parents use excessive punishment and chronic nagging, they themselves can destroy the self-concept of their own children. The notion that parents have the power to build self-confidence and self-esteem within their own children was always well received as a wonderful "new" idea.

In my *Communique'* article about parents of handicapped children, I described the following five myths common to many service providers, all of which I had learned from my own experiences as a special parent.

• Myth No. 1: *The guilt feelings held by parents of handicapped children should be the primary and immediate concern.* The truth of the matter is that parents who are faced with the reality of having a handicapped child do not experience guilt primarily, if ever. They do suffer from a variety of other feelings: shock, disbelief, fear, anger, sadness, shame, and rejection. I then explained simple strategies for uncovering the current status of the parent.

• Myth No. 2: *The possibility that the parent is responsible for the child's problem is great, or at least that parenting skills are very poor.* Yes, it can happen that a parent, through neglect and abuse, may have contributed to the seriousness of a child's disability. However, if a parent leaves a team meeting with new feelings of unfounded guilt, that session was a failure. Furthermore, it becomes destructive when team members structure a relationship with a parent based on false and preconceived parental blame.

• Myth No. 3: *The worst of all things is for the parent to fail to face, immediately, the full reality of a child's disability.* For some reason it is common among both professional and lay people to express anger at parents who block out the disorders of their children, which are obvious to others. In truth, it is cruel to demand acceptance of severe trauma in one's child that could be accepted more easily in small doses.

• Myth No. 4: *What the parent needs and wants most from the examiner is sympathy.* Certainly, pity by itself is not constructive. Rather, there is never any situation where one cannot find something nice to say, and it is always effective to acknowledge any parental strength the parent may have demonstrated. The parent of a child with Down's Syndrome once wisely described her son in these terms: "What happened to my child is tragic, but he himself is not a tragedy." Moreover, I liked to convey to the parents that although they face many challenges, greater obstacles have been overcome.

- Myth No. 5: *When the damage, disability or affliction appears to be irreversible, a picture of despair is the only recourse.* I always like to remind parents and team members that despite the strides made in the last hundred years in diagnosing and treating the disabled, future research will reveal undreamed of avenues of new helpful strategies. Revealing to parents that we do not yet have all of the best answers offers some comfort. It can serve as a vehicle for restoring order and control into a parent's world, which has become disordered and chaotic.

Over the years I had opportunities to meet so many parents, some with disabilities of their own. Some of these encounters proved to be frustrating for me, since I was not always in a position to be helpful.

There were parents who were seriously hearing impaired, and who required "signing" in order for them to understand the proceedings of the meetings. One such couple, both of whom were college educated and gainfully employed, were the proud parents of two children. Their daughter suffered from a mild hearing loss, and their son, who had been evaluated by me, had a learning disability. In the course of my evaluating and interviewing the learning disabled boy, one of my routine questions was: "If you could change anything in your life, what would you change?" I was dismayed when he responded, "I would change my parents!" As this was the only time I had ever heard a child allege such thoughts, I asked him to elaborate. "Yes," he repeated, "I wish that I had different parents!" I was not in a position to probe or counsel his allegation, but each time I met these parents at a meeting, a sadness for this family passed through me.

On another occasion, I reported the results of my evaluation of a learning disabled girl to a mother who was legally blind. During our conference, she observed, "You really love your work, don't you?" I was flattered that this sightless mother noted my pleasure just from hearing my voice and responded "Yes, I do!"

In addition to the vision and hearing impaired parents, infrequently a parent confined to a wheel chair appeared at one of the meetings. These were not the parents who were the most challenging at meetings, however. For the most part, these parents with handicaps of their own were always pleasant and cheerful.

It was the parent who felt his child's special needs were not being serviced properly who displayed the most frustration and anger at meetings. The most tormented parent I had ever observed was the agonized mother of a hearing impaired child, distressed with a team placement decision. She had a full tantrum at a meeting, in which she began banging her fist against a wall and screaming, "You people never give the kind of help which is needed. My child needs a class which will really help him!" Perhaps only a parent who had suffered a similar frustration could identify with the anguish of this woman.

The couple who put forth the greatest effort to receive desired services for their legally blind child actually sold their house to move closer to my school which had a special program for vision-impaired children. When their son was only a pre-schooler, he was stricken with eye cancer, which resulted in the loss of his vision. By the time he reached first grade his parents were determined that he remain in his regular classroom setting, rather than be placed in the "School for the Blind."

The boy's teachers agreed that he was a pleasant, well-liked child, of above-average potential, yet there was a long list of specialists required to service his needs: teachers of braille, mobility (handling himself both in the classroom and out of doors), physical therapy, and occupational therapy. Regular team meetings to review his progress would have at least fifteen people seated around the conference table. It was most impressive that he did succeed in this non-handicapped placement, and that it was made possible by the extensive research and monitoring of his parents.

I must not fail to mention that I also have met parents who had been ruining their families through some destructive addiction of their own. Although these parents were totally absorbed and disoriented by their enslavement to drugs, it is a fallacy to assume that any parents, even these, are totally indifferent to the progress of their children in school. On the contrary, I have observed that no matter how limited, deprived, or dysfunctional any parent was, I never met one who did not glow upon hearing of their child's progress, no matter how small.

It was my practice, after evaluating a child, to always try to meet privately with the parent prior to the team meeting. In this way, I hoped to avoid any chance of shocking them when presenting some unsettling news. I would tell them exactly what I would be saying at the meeting, and ask point blank, "This is what I am going to say, are you comfortable with that?" No matter how hopeless a child's condition appeared to be, it had always been my focus to create a supportive, optimistic, and productive conference for the parent. It is difficult for anyone to realize how emotionally uplifting it is for a parent to hear anything positive about a very damaged child. In fact, I could never write a evaluation report without listing the child's strengths, no matter how trivial.

This procedure worked like a charm with hundreds of parents, with few exceptions. During my private conference with one of these couples, I had the challenging task of explaining to them that their child was intellectually limited. The mother was the spokesperson, while her husband spoke only minimally. I went through my usual routine of describing the strengths and weakness of their child, and I told them specifically what I would be reporting at the meeting. I explained that if they had any problems with the diagnosis, we should discuss them privately.

So, when we finally sat at the meeting and I gave my report, I was shocked at the mother's response. She berated me and everyone else present at the meeting for saying these offensive things about her child. But, what really hurt was that she appeared to have deceived me with clever deliberation. This was the only time that any parent had done this, and the team and I were totally taken by surprise.

Diametrically opposite to these sly parents, was another surprising couple, whose view of my work with their ten-year-old son differed vastly. Their son had severe learning and behavior problems, and was evaluated and treated for a number of years at a well-known clinic in Baltimore. The clinic had diagnosed their child as "emotionally disturbed" due to poor parenting and, sadly, these parents had suffered for years through their guilt and confusion.

When I evaluated the boy, my results differed significantly from those of the clinic. I discovered that his primary handicap was "moderate mental retardation." When I reported my results to the parents, tears of relief rolled down the mother's cheeks and the father almost smiled! After their long siege through the misdiagnosis by the clinic, the mother sobbed: "We've thought for some time that we could not be to blame for his weaknesses! We are so relieved to know you agree with us!" These parents were probably the only ones I was ever to see who were actually happy to learn that their child was intellectually limited.

It was quite common for some team members to describe many parents of handicapped children as "defensive," "quarrelsome," or even "manipulative." But I liked to stress to my team members that what each of these parents was really trying to say is, "I hurt inside; please help me!"

In later years I came to believe that my "hidden agenda" was not much of a secret to other team members. What pleased me most was when they followed my lead and changed their own manner with the parents.

I was most gratified with the response of a team member when we were faced with a particularly difficult parental situation. Her words were "Let Thelma explain it to the parent – she does it best!"

CHAPTER TWENTY

Remarkable Partners

No office can dignify a man,
but many a man dignifies his office.

Leo Rosten

Colleagues played an integral role in my happy but sometimes tumultuous days in the Baltimore Schools. Those with whom I connected most were the speech pathologists, social workers, and principals. A fondness developed with many of them that was deep and lasting.

Speech pathologists were the group with whom I probably had the closest contact. Although the bulk of their work involved direct therapy with children, they played an integral role with team decisions. I could observe first hand the great service they rendered with remediating speech and language difficulties. Upon reaching middle school, the fortunate special education students who had received speech and language therapy during elementary school had an academic edge over peers who did not. The speech therapists were fortunate that the fruits of their labor were visible, and I gave them my most enthusiastic applause.

Yet, friction was often created between us at screening meetings in which we were directed only to order one evaluation for each student, either by the school psychologist or the speech pathologist. At times when each group was understaffed and each was trying in desperation to lower its swamped case loads, bickering could develop.

Most difficult were the few speech pathologists who had assumed the erroneous view that serious emotional disturbance was prevalent in many of their students. This was distressing, since only the school psychologist was deemed qualified to examine this not-too-common but very time consuming disorder.

However, the question of emotional disturbance, once raised, could never be ignored, I was regularly on guard for three factors pointing to dangers: "Might the child harm himself? Might he harm others?" or "Might he destroy property?" After screening these issues thoroughly with every referred student, I felt I could make a judgment about which children required a full evaluation by a psychologist. But there was no convincing the few speech pathologists who deemed one child after another – in demanding, tearful voices – as possibly having this rare disorder. Fortunately, the majority of the speech pathologists saw eye to eye with me.

The school social workers were another group with whom I worked closely. I was always impressed with their uncanny skills in "sniffing out" those families where drugs and other deviances were prevalent. Of course this was vital, since the tragic outcome of drug-dependence usually damaged the entire family.

By the nature of their responsibilities, social workers were gatherers of major confidential information. Recording this information and sharing it with others was more important than some of them realized, and withholding it could prove problematic for me. Once, early in my career, when I reported to a team the results of my evaluation with a first grader, I stated, "There is more going on with this child than I know, and I feel that critical information is missing." To my surprise, the social worker who had worked with the family revealed just that pertinent information, "Oh yes, his mother is a diagnosed schizophrenic, and she has been in and out of institutions since he was born."

On another occasion, withholding information proved to be quite damaging. A fourteen-year-old girl had been referred to me because of her withdrawn and quarrelsome behavior. Records revealed that her biological mother had died a few years before, leaving her maternal grandmother as the legal guardian of five children. The grandmother proved to be a diligent care-giver, and a hard working woman who was employed as a custodian at one of the elementary schools. She was a careful manager and was able to purchase the house where she lived with the children.

When I gave this girl a full battery of intellectual and personality tests, there were clear indications that her contact with reality was profoundly weak. Even though she was described by others as a loner who communicated little with peers, she viewed herself as a popular girl much sought after by both boys and girls. And she related to me one crucial piece of information, which no one else had reported.

I was astounded when she told me that while she was at home alone one day someone had thrown a firebomb into their basement window. The home was sufficiently damaged so that she and her family were now living in temporary quarters. Even though she was on the case load of a social worker, whose report I had read carefully, there was no indication of any fire or relocation of living quarters.

In any event, I diagnosed her as an adolescent who needed psychiatric intervention as soon as possible, and I invited her grandmother to a private conference. She was most cooperative and arrived promptly at the hour designated. The grandmother told me that upon the death of her daughter, this grandchild had the most difficulty adjusting. She welcomed my advice that more intensive, urgent therapy was needed than the school could supply, and she was most receptive when we set up an appointment at a local hospital. At that point I felt relief that we had identified the grave urgency of this troubled child's problem and were moving in the right direction.

Alas, one morning several weeks later, as I read the Baltimore Sun over my breakfast coffee, I spotted an article that sent shock waves through me. Throughout my years with the Baltimore City schools, there was always a chronic fear that one day, belatedly, I would learn of some horrible event relating to one of my clients. This was it! In the newspaper article, where no name was given because of her age, a fourteen-year-old girl was described as being detained by juvenile authorities for setting fire to three of her residences, one following the other. My heart sank as I realized quickly that this was my client who had claimed that she was home alone when the first residence was fire bombed.

I couldn't help but wonder and bemoan why the event of the first fire was not reported in writing somewhere in the girl's recent records. This event led me to write an essay for the *Communiqué* which I titled, "The School Psychologist as a Detective." I hoped to convey to others the importance of both reporting all information, and of examining every piece of information available, just as a detective must do.

The most remarkable of my partners were the school principals. It is true that earlier in this book I related tales of the few who offended me, but for the most part, it was my privilege to be working with these "commanders of the ship," these "bosses" at the schools.

I was in total awe of the obligations that they shouldered for the safety of hundreds of children. If any misstep involving a student or staff member occurred, the news media were quick to place the blame squarely on the principal. In addition, principals also supervised teachers, custodial and other staff, placated disgruntled parents, approved building repairs, and served as an occasional school nurse. I used to think that if I were to awaken one morning and discover I was a principal, "How could I possibly handle an entire school?"

Yet, my relationships with the principals could be described as a roller coaster ride. For the most part, I was favored by them with esteem, warmth, and affection. On the other hand, I have been ignored, offended, and even blamed for not correcting the foibles of other colleagues. There have been days when I did nothing special beyond my job description, and was treated as though I had saved the world. On other occasions, I could give eons of overtime far beyond the call of duty, only to find it was not noticed in any way.

I was most astonished when these overworked principals found time for extra projects. As an example, I was able to observe one of them, Janet Merritt, as she worked on an original project, that of preparing fourth and fifth graders for an oratorical contest. As it happened, the computer with which I sometimes worked was located in the teachers' lounge where the practice sessions took place and thus, I had a private viewing of her didactic lessons in elocution and of her development of the blossoming future speakers.

Having witnessed the rehearsals in progress, I was filled with special pride as I listened on the day of the contest, to the dynamic readings and watched the theatrical performances that the talented students delivered.

When I first entered the Baltimore Schools, my African American friends – who were older than I – had grown up in the days of Jim Crow. In those days, as friendships deepened, they confided tales of the humiliation and hardship which they suffered through segregation.

In contrast to the past, the stories confided by my new, younger, non-white friends were often positive, pleasant stories. For instance, one of the speech pathologists told me one day that her father, an administrator, would be observing at the school.

She then went on to tell of the courtship of her parents. Years back, her grandfather was president of a college in the South, a school for black students. Alas, when her mother, daughter of the president, began dating her father, he was employed as a garbage hauler. Her distinguished grandparents, appalled with their daughter's choice, tried to discourage the match. However, my friend's mother, recognizing the talents of her handsome young man, persisted. Her confidence in him was rewarded, and her choice of mate worked his way up the ladder to a successful career in the educational system.

Another speech pathologist told a heart rending, extraordinary story of her first meeting with her husband. It seems my friend had been shopping on a Saturday evening with her cousin at the supermarket. While there, she caught the eye of a handsome young man, who was immediately smitten with her. He begged in vain for her phone number, but she was too proper to reveal it to a complete stranger. However, she did tell him her name, which he stored carefully in his mind.

Some time later, this young man, who taught art at a public school, became acquainted with a substitute teacher there. Surprisingly, the substitute had the same last name as the pretty girl he was unable to forget. Taking a gamble, he asked his new acquaintance if he knew my friend. She was his niece! However, the substitute teacher could not remember his niece's exact address, only the name of her street. Her dauntless admirer located the street, then knocked on doors searching for her. When he located her house, my friend was not at home, although her mother was. Her mother, who also taught school, was immediately taken with him, and encouraged the friendship. The romance which followed led to a most contented and successful marriage. This story's aftermath makes the unlikely role of her uncle unforgettable. After spending only one day as a substitute at her husband's school, he passed away, sadly, the following week. It is easy to believe that Divine providence was at work here!

My experiences in the schools as the only Jewish person, and a Sabbath observer at that, were often interesting. Although most of my colleagues were highly supportive, there were a minimal number who behaved differently. There was a Miss Casey, a nurse who was a staunch believer in her religion, who never missed an opportunity, albeit slyly, to try to convert me to her beliefs. I enjoyed chatting with her otherwise, but after her shrewd approach one day, I was forced to respond: "Miss Casey, if you wish to remain my friend, you must never say anything like that to me again!" She followed my directive faithfully, and our friendship grew.

Another colleague asked me pointedly, in the presence of others at a team meeting, if I shared a particular religious belief of importance to her. My swift but congenial response, "Oh, I make it a practice never to discuss religion or politics in the work place!" was effective. Needless to say, it was the strength of knowing who I am, Jewishly, which made my replies effective.

At the same time, the support of most of my colleagues was such that a Jewish colleague, who was not observant, made this observation: "You know, the principals have a higher regard for you, greater than they do for me. They really respect your sincere dedication as a Sabbath observer!"

Given that this was true, it still was difficult for them to understand that I followed laws for eating only kosher food. Principals who occasionally served catered breakfasts, and sometimes lunch to their staff, seemed offended when I did not really participate. One social worker, who liked to bring her home-baked goods to meetings, was angered when I did not eat her cakes. In fact, once when I brought some home-made popcorn, she pointedly avoided it, saying, "No, I cannot eat anything Thelma brought. She never touches my food!"

At the same time, in later years as kosher restaurants became more popular in Baltimore, my situation became easier. It became possible to guide a group to such a kosher eatery, and it was then that understanding of the kosher laws grew. For instance, when one of the Dunkin Donuts shops in the neighborhood received kosher supervision, these donuts were seen frequently at meetings. I was amused one day when a box of Dunkin donuts appeared on a table at a meeting and as I walked over to look at the box, one of my collegues said quickly, "Mrs. Blumberg, those donuts are not for you!" The boxes were not labeled, and she knew I would not know that these came from one of the non-kosher Dunkin Donuts stores.

The friendships of my remarkable partners were dear to me, and they left an indelible, pleasing aura in my heart. They contributed to the fact that my happy days with the school system greatly outnumbered the troubled ones.

CHAPTER TWENTY-ONE

The Miracle, the Children

Each child brings his own blessing into the world.
Leo Rosten

A counselor for the elderly once told me that the fulfillment which she received from helping her clients fell within the range of a religious experience. I could easily identify with her feelings. Because I viewed each child as a unique creation, I felt privileged when I was able to explore the almost mystic foundations of each. I felt that whatever productive role I might then play in improving their lives rendered me a veritable partner in their creation.

Among my young clients, there were children whose problems fell into many categories. So many were sad, others interesting in their rarity, and to my utmost pleasure, many made me laugh.

To the surprise of many people outside the school system, I never personally encountered any child who behaved in an overtly violent manner with me. I have found that the most troubled child enjoys the security of a one-to-one counseling situation such as mine. Furthermore, it was my feeling that fears of danger from the behavior of children in the city schools were too often exaggerated. As long as twenty-five years ago, when my car was in the shop for repairs, I had occasion to take a taxi to one of my southeast Baltimore middle schools. The friendly driver, a tall burly man, yelled out, upon leaving me off, "Lady, you've got more courage than I do. I wouldn't want to go into that building!"

The most frightening child I had ever encountered was a reportedly scary twelve-year-old sixth grader. He had made violent threats to his teacher, the principal, and even the school secretary, and all of them genuinely feared him. As I was scheduled to evaluate him, the staff members were all concerned with my safety. We made all kinds of plans, setting up a comfortable place with magazines right outside the door of my office, where his mother could sit and guard me, if needed.

As it happened, his mother didn't even show up at the appointed time. However, when he was brought from his classroom, he followed suit with all the other "rough" children I had seen: he seemed to immensely enjoy that I had some positive things to tell him about himself. Perhaps he was one of those children who had never heard anyone say anything nice to him before. Afterward, I was most complimented when he told the secretary that he wished I could be his teacher. When parents and teachers understand that these misbehaving children cry for a "boost-up" of self-concept, they too reap rewards.

Of course, there were specially trained crisis teams for the rare emergency occasions, made up of volunteer social workers and psychologists. One Friday at lunch time, I found myself in the Central Office. Although I was not an official member of the crisis team, an emergency arose while I was there, and I was summoned to a nearby high school. Sadly, a boy had just drowned in an indoor swimming pool. Not trained to serve on the crisis team, I was unreasonably nervous about the extent of my inadequacy.

When I arrived there, someone had already begun to guide groups of ten students into different rooms, each with a counselor, in order to ease the shock of the students who observed the drowning. Thus, I was immediately ushered into a small room with a group. Instinctively, I had each of my students relate, one by one, what had been observed, their reactions, and what we could do now. When we were half-way through, the door of the small room opened and there stood a very concerned Central Office administrator, checking on the progress of my group. To my satisfaction and relief, after she left one of the girls reacted quickly and in anger, saying, "We were doing so well! Why did she come in and break the spell?"

Probably the rarest clients on my case load were those children who carried a disability of "elective mutism." Such children speak only to the family at home and to playmates on the street, but never utter a word to the teacher or peers in the classroom. This condition is so rare that few school psychologists ever get to see it. In my quarter-century of experience, I worked with three of these children and felt the problem required more clinical service than a school could offer as there were gross misconceptions and little knowledge about it in a typical school staff. It is a very stubborn and difficult-to-treat disorder, and I felt that it would be most productive if I advised staff members about the strengths, weaknesses, and distinctiveness of each child. Still, as with many other conditions of low incidence, much remains to be learned in terms of treating these cases.

The first of these children, a girl who attended a Jewish Day School, was first evaluated by me at age five and that time she did speak to me, answering questions to the best of her ability. It was then my sad responsibility to inform the parents that her level of functioning fell within the mild range of intellectual limitation, with an IQ between 55 and 65.

I was to meet this child again three years later, when she was transferred to a special education class at my school. Although there were many conversations with her teacher prior to the evaluation, the fact that she never spoke was not mentioned. Nowhere was it documented. It was therefore a great shock to learn that sometime within the recent three years, she had stopped speaking outside of the home. Such a child would make any dedicated teacher feel overwhelmed and helpless. Furthermore, there were always unfounded misconceptions by staff members that these children were abused at home. It frustrated me that the best help I could offer was to refer the parents to an outside specialized clinic, dispel misconceptions of the teachers, and to offer teaching directives geared to her specific strengths and weaknesses.

The two other clients who suffered from elective mutism were a pair of identical, handsome, well-developed twin boys. Reportedly they were very aggressive with peers. They were very similar intellectually and matched each other in terms of total withdrawal from speaking to anyone in the classroom. Having followed them from ages seven to ten, I was pleased that, as they learned to read and write, I was able to interview them by having them put in writing their answers to my questions. The volume of information that I could gain about their memories, fears, and wishes by this method was gratifying and helpful.

The saddest of all my young clients were the foster children. They were most often victims of traumatic and damaging emotional and physical treatment, usually occurring within their birth homes. As it happened, over the years there was one major change which took place within some Baltimore City families, the increase of parental substance abuse and this seemed to be the most harmful factor toward damaging children. When I entered the system twenty-five years ago, our team, upon learning of a pre-school foster child who had been a victim of any injurious treatment inflicted at their birth home, would sit around the table and lament for the poor child. However, a quarter-century later, as these sad children became more commonplace, there was less time to grieve over each case.

Nothing demonstrates this decline better than my quite recent visit to a pre-school special education class. I was surprised to see a little boy there who had no hair growing on the entire top center part of his head, only on the sides and back. Assuming that this was the result of a birth defect, I was shocked when his teacher told me that his drug crazed mother had attacked him with an ax.

I became quite acquainted with another child, an eleven year old foster daughter of a retired teacher. Reportedly a victim of physical and sexual abuse, her shield of defenses was so strong and so difficult to penetrate, that when she spoke of her biological family, she referred to them as "my people." The best I could do was to offer nurturing support and to help with reading and spelling skills.

Among the most apparent cases of physical abuse with which I had worked, was a child with hands permanently damaged and scarred from burns. It seems that a "care giver" had held up her hands to a gas flame as a means of punishment.

But there was one thing which was most surprising. Despite the pain and suffering which these children experienced, it would be rare to meet a foster child who did not long to be reunited with his biological parents.

Along side all of this sadness, it was fortunate for me that there were so many students who made me laugh. The things they said and did in innocence were often so precious and so comical. As an example, there was one little seven-year-old girl whom I had evaluated, and who was probably one of the most hyperactive children I had ever seen. I kept my cool throughout the ninety minute session, never scolding or raising my voice to her, regardless of how many times she left her seat or asked irrelevant questions. Upon completion, I sensed she was feeling comfortable, and was probably wondering why I didn't ever correct or scold her as did all other adults. I was taken aback by her next words, "There is something I want to tell you, but I am afraid to, because it will make you angry." My interest piqued, I responded, "Children tell me all sorts of things and I never get angry with them." "Oh, no!", she declared emphatically, "I can't tell you this." Suspecting her secret had something to do with my being white, I asked point blank if it did. She then blurted out, "I think all white people look like mayonnaise!"

Among my amusing students was a twelve-year-old clever, but learning disabled, middle school boy. He was new to the school, and the special education department head, not realizing that he had recently been tested, asked me to conduct a new re-evaluation. Halfway through, I could see the speed with which he responded to all of my complicated puzzle pieces and questions, and I asked if he had ever seen these materials before. "Oh yes" he responded, "Many times. And you do this very well!"

Some years back, I was in the process of administering a group self-concept test to an entire class of seventh graders. From the back of the classroom, I heard a boy comment, "She looks like Mrs. Munster." (Mrs. Munster was a funny, weird-looking white witch from a situation comedy of that era.) Luckily I felt confident enough about the way I looked to really laugh.

Another of my schools was located in a neighborhood where the children have little opportunity to see white people. One day as I sat opposite a seven-year-old boy at my examination table, he began stroking my hand, very gently. Puzzled by this at first, I was surprised and amused when he said, "You're white!" More recently, another boy from that school sitting in the same seat looked into my face and declared "You're old!" I smiled and responded quickly, "Yes, I am a grandmother."

A couple of years after I retired from the Baltimore City Schools, I was invited back to work on a temporary basis, not working with children directly, but only to attend team meetings. One day when I arrived at my school, the regularly assigned psychologist surprised me by saying that she was suffering from such back pain that she couldn't handle an emergency evaluation of that day. I could not refuse, and proceeded with the evaluation, using her materials. These were arranged more neatly than mine used to be, but differently, and I did not have all of my own interview and reporting props with me. Thus the evaluation took me a half-hour longer than I felt that it should.

I was feeling very frustrated and uncomfortable about this, until the very end. As my little nine-year-old student was leaving the room and was half-way to the door, he turned around and walked back towards me. His hands were outstretched, to give me a farewell hug. This was a wonderful reminder of what my career had been all about.

And, now, as I reside in retirement in Kiryat Arba, the fond memories of my tale of "agony and ecstasy" at the schools remain with me. My story may be likened to the seasons of Kiryat Arba, where the unique weather – six months of daily beautiful blue skies and sunshine – contrasts with six months of unpredictable rain. Yet, no one there ever complains on the wet, stormy days. Instead, this is a time of rejoicing for answered prayers for rain!

By the same token, turbulence at my schools could never diminish the fascination of my days there. Nor could it interfere with my innate love for the captivating children. Rather, it magnifies and completes my tale, No Time For Lunch!

Thelma Alpert Blumberg renders testing to a Baltimore student.

Thelma Alpert Blumberg counseling a Baltimore student

Committee for Exploring needs in the schools:
L to R – Jim Constantinides, Chairperson Mary Reid, Carol
Sobelman, Thelma Blumberg

Levy Van Leeuwen, school psychologist, Kiryat Arba

Talmud Torah serviced by psychologist Van Leeuwen,
Kiryat Arba

Ulpana girls high school serviced by psychologist Van
Leeuwen

Thelma Alpert Blumberg's grandson socializes with a
newly arrived group of Ethiopian children in Kiryat Arba

Thelma Alpert Blumberg and two Ethiopian boys, Kiryat Arba